THE
CONSTITUTION
OF
INDIA
SIMPLIFIED

THE
CONSTITUTION
OF
INDIA
SIMPLIFIED

BY

ANMOL SINGH

&

G.B. SINGH

SOVEREIGN STAR
PUBLISHING

Sovereign Star Publishing, Inc
PO Box 392
Lathrop, CA 95330
United States of America
www.sovstar.com

ISBN-13: 978-0-9814992-8-4 (paper)
ISBN-10: 0-9814992-8-7 (paper)

We dedicate this book to the people of India,
who have been deprived
of their democratic and human rights,
and to the memory of M.N. Roy.

Contents

List of Figures

x

Figure A: Front Page of the Original Constitution of India

Foreword

Those of us who were born and raised in India after 1947 heard in vague terms about its Constitution. I did not know anyone who had read the Constitution or even seen what it looked like. Years later, when I enquired with the "India specialist" posted at the U.S. Department of State, I found that he had not seen a copy of the Constitution, let alone read it. But back in India, my friends and I held a fond inkling that the Constitution existed and guided the workings of the Indian political system. As a student in India, I had no doubt that its Constitution must be a glow of light in the arena of documents at the global scale extolling the virtues of liberal democracy. However, by the time I completed college there, some doubts had crept in—but there was nobody on the horizon from whom to seek answers. Strangely, nobody knew the answers, and nobody other than I enquired.

In the 1970s, I migrated to the United States. In the United States, my yearning to know the mystery surrounding the Constitution of India intensified, and in 1991, I was able to procure a hard copy of it. Nothing had prepared me to face the reality jotted in its pages. This book is a result of many years of analysis of this document and the recognition that the Constitution is so verbose, and conflict ridden that it needs simplification for a common person to be able to comprehend it. Because the welfare of a common man is directly affected, it becomes important for the people of India to understand what the Constitution is about.

The prospective reader will gain a lot from reading this book and walk away reassessing what transpired in the fabrication of the Constitution, its enactment, and the last 68 years of its exercise as an authority over the people of India. Another issue is the role of Dr. B.R. Ambedkar (the famous leader of India's Untouchables[1] , also called Dalits), who has been promoted all along as the "Father of the Indian Constitution," "Architect of the Indian Constitution," or "one of the architects," etc. In addition, on the compound surrounding the Indian Parliament building, there stands a statue of Dr. Ambedkar holding a copy of the Constitution. Is this depiction of history accurate? Or are we being spoon fed the false narrative of the history of the Constituent Assembly (which met from December 9, 1946 to January 24, 1950) from whose deliberations this Constitution came into fruition? During the period of these deliberations, Dr. Ambedkar held the position of chair of the Drafting Committee.

In this book, we have deliberately examined only those features of the Constitution which are pertinent to the essential functions of governance (by the government) combined with the fundamental rights we hear from the propagandists that this Constitution has bestowed upon the citizens of India. Join Anmol Singh and myself in this exploration!

G.B. Singh

Introduction to India's Constitution

Sir, looking back on the work of the Constituent Assembly it will now be two years, eleven months and seventeen days since it first met on the 9th of December 1946. During this period the Constituent Assembly has altogether held eleven sessions. Out of these eleven sessions the first six were spent in passing the Objectives Resolution and the consideration of the Reports of Committees on Fundamental Rights, on Union Constitution, on Union Powers, on Provincial Constitution, on Minorities and on the Scheduled Areas and Scheduled Tribes. The seventh, eighth, ninth, tenth and the eleventh sessions were devoted to the consideration of the Draft Constitution. These eleven sessions of the Constituent Assembly have consumed 165 days. Out of these, the Assembly spent 114 days for the consideration of the Draft Constitution.

—B.R. Ambedkar
Constituent Assembly Debates
Vol. XI, November 25, 1949

The Constitution of India is voluminous, inconsistent, contradictory, cumbersome, and therefore often unreadable. Besides being the longest written constitution, it is promoted internationally in the bigger context in which India sits as the "world's largest democracy." The Constitution as of 2017 is composed of 395 articles, 12 schedules, and 3 appendices. The amendment count, to date, has reached 101. Apologists describe it as "sacred," implying God ordained it, and promoting it with reverence to other younger politicians and people at large.

After the Preamble, and leaving aside the schedules and appendices, its layout is spread out in twenty-two parts under the following headings:

	Preamble
Part I	The Union and its territory
Part II	Citizenship
Part III	Fundamental Rights
Part IVA	Fundamental Duties
Part V	The Union
Part VI	The States
Part VII	(Repealed by Const. (Seventh Amendment) Act, 1956)
Part VIII	The Union Territories
Part IX	The Panchayats
Part IXA	The Municipalies
Part IXB	The Cooperative Societies
Part X	The Scheduled and Tribal Areas
Part XI	Relations between the Union and the States
Part XII	Finance, Property, Conracts and Suits

Part XIII	Trade, Commerce and Intercourse within the Territory of India
Part XIV	Services under the Union and the States
Part XV	Elections
Part XVI	Special Provisions relating to certain Classes
Part XVII	Official Language
Part XVIII	Emergency Provisions
Part XIX	Miscellaneous
Part XX	Amendment of the Constitution
Part XXI	Temporary, Transitional and Special Provision
Part XXII	Short Title, Commencement, Authoritative Text in Hindi and Repeals

The general structure of the Indian Constitution is such that one article is practically invalidated by a later article, and one clause is invalidated by another clause and so on. Another common pattern is that an article makes room for an exception which a subsequent article exploits. This results in confusion, to say the least.

The approach charted in this book attempts to minimize the confusion. We have grouped together the differently spaced articles to bring the profundity of the issue at hand to the attention of the reader.

This book is spread out in six chapters, followed by the Conclusion and five appendices. Chapter 1 focuses on the fundamental rights enumerated in the Constitution. The reader will get the opportunity to read the entire gamut of these "rights." Chapter 2 takes a selective and closer look at those articles of the Constitution dealing with the Government of India in New Delhi. Chapter 3 directs its scrutiny at the governmental structures at the State level. Likewise, Chapter 4 probes the Union Territories administered by the Government of India. Chapter 5 focuses on the emergency provisions, a punitive tool in the hands of Indian leaders. Chapter 6 is quite different. The role of *Modern Hinduism* in the affairs of India has often escaped critical inquiry. The Conclusion assembles the often-forgotten historical bits dealing with Dr. Ambedkar, M.N. Roy, Mohandas K. Gandhi, and Dyarchy. In the appendix sections—specifically appendices C, D, and E—the reader will see for the first time those illustrations that beautified the pages of the original copy of the Constitution of India.[2]

1

Fundamental Rights

The task of the Drafting Committee would have been a very difficult one if this Constituent Assembly has been merely a motley crowd, a tasseleted pavement without cement, a black stone here and a white stone there in which each member or each group was a law unto itself. There would have been nothing but chaos. This possibility of chaos was reduced to nil by the existence of the Congress Party inside the Assembly which brought into its proceedings a sense of order and discipline. It is because of the discipline of the Congress Party that the Drafting Committee was able to pilot the Constitution in the Assembly with the sure knowledge as to the fate of each article and each amendment. The Congress Party is, therefore, entitled to all the credit for the smooth sailing of the Draft Constitution in the Assembly.

—B.R. Ambedkar
Constituent Assembly Debates
Vol. XI. November 25, 1949

It seems to be suggested that those who made the Constitution had no sense, that fundamental rights must be elastic, that they must leave enough room for progressive changes. I must, Sir, as the Chairman of the Drafting Committee, repudiate any such suggestion. Anyone, who reads the fundamental rights as they are enacted in the Constitution, will find that every fundamental right has got an exception.

—B.R. Ambedkar
March 19, 1955, Rajya Sabha

Fundamental rights are essential to the healthy functioning of a democracy. If the citizens have no rights to form and express opinions, then they are vulnerable to manipulation by the State, and the fundamental right to vote freely becomes questionable. In addition, with no constitutional limits on State power, it becomes difficult to accept that the State represents the collective will of its citizens. Without freedom of the individual, there cannot be a democracy as envisioned in the West. In this chapter, we will investigate whether the Indian Constitution provides any fundamental rights. Before continuing, we recommend reading carefully the entire "Fundamental Rights" portion of the Constitution of India which has been reproduced in Appendix A.

The provisions related to fundamental rights are contained in Part III (articles 12 through 35) of the Constitution. Article 19 seems to provide the citizens with the right to free speech, expression, and peaceful assembly. However, all these rights are subject to arbitrary limitations in the interests of "public order," "decency," "morality," "national integrity," and so on.

19. (1) All citizens shall have the right—

(a) to freedom of speech and expression;

(b) to assemble peaceably and without arms;

(c) to form associations or unions;

(d) to move freely throughout the territory of India;

(e) to reside and settle in any part of the territory of India; and

(g) to practise any profession, or to carry on any occupation, trade or business.

(2) Nothing in sub-clause (a) of clause (1) shall affect the operation of any existing law, or prevent the State from making any law, in so far as such law imposes reasonable restrictions on the exercise of the right conferred by the said sub-clause in the interests of the sovereignty and integrity of India, the security of the State, friendly relations with foreign States, public order, decency or morality, or in relation to contempt of court, defamation or incitement to

an offence.

(3) Nothing in sub-clause (b) of the said clause shall affect the operation of any existing law in so far as it imposes, or prevent the State from making any law imposing, in the interests of the sovereignty and integrity of India or public order, reasonable restrictions on the exercise of the right conferred by the said sub-clause.

(4) Nothing in sub-clause (c) of the said clause shall affect the operation of any existing law in so far as it imposes, or prevent the State from making any law imposing, in the interests of the sovereignty and integrity of India or public order or morality, reasonable restrictions on the exercise of the right conferred by the said sub-clause.

(5) Nothing in sub-clauses (d) and (e) of the said clause shall affect the operation of any existing law in so far as it imposes, or prevent the State from making any law imposing, reasonable restrictions on the exercise of any of the rights conferred by the said sub-clauses either in the interests of the general public or for the protection of the interests of any Scheduled Tribe.

(6) Nothing in sub-clause (g) of the said clause shall affect the operation of any existing law in so far as it imposes, or prevent the State from making any law imposing, in the interests of the general public, reasonable restrictions on the exercise of the right conferred by the said sub-clause, and, in particular, nothing in the said sub-clause shall affect the operation of any existing law in so far as it relates to, or prevent the State from making any law relating to,–

—

(i) the professional or technical qualifications necessary for practising any profession or carrying on any occupation, trade or business, or

(ii) the carrying on by the State, or by a corporation owned or controlled by the State, of any trade, business, industry or service, whether to the exclusion, complete or partial, of citizens or otherwise.

The provision related to the freedom of religion, which is embodied in Article 25, is no different.

25. (1) Subject to public order, morality and health and to the other provisions of this Part, all persons are equally entitled to freedom of conscience and the right freely to profess, practise and propagate religion.

(2) Nothing in this article shall affect the operation of any existing law or prevent the State from making any law—

(a) regulating or restricting any economic, financial, political or other secular activity which may be associated with religious practice;

(b) providing for social welfare and reform or the throwing open of Hindu religious institutions of a public character to all classes and sections of Hindus.

Explanation I.—The wearing and carrying of *kirpans* shall be deemed to be included in the profession of the Sikh religion.

Explanation II.—In sub-clause (b) of clause (2), the reference to Hindus shall be construed as including a reference to persons professing the Sikh, Jaina or Buddhist religion, and the reference to Hindu religious institutions shall be construed accordingly.

Judging from the angle of guarantee and certainty, it appears that the Constitution does not offer any fundamental rights[3]. The exceptions to which these rights are subject are so loose that those in power easily manipulate them at the expense of the citizens who deserve guaranteed rights to protect themselves from the arbitrary intrusion of the State. Basically, the Constitution provides us with rights in one article and then takes them back in sub-clauses or subsequent articles. Article 19 is the best example of this.

A good example of guaranteed and unambiguous fundamental rights is the First Amendment to the Constitution of the United States.

Amendment I. Congress shall make no law respecting an establishment of religion, or prohibiting the free exercise thereof; or abridging the freedom of speech, or of the press, or the right of the people peaceably to assemble, and to petition the Government for a redress of grievances.

[No futher qualifiers]

We ask the reader to read the Appendix B to grasp the quandary of fundamental rights of the Constitution of India.

Now let us show you how easy it is to manipulate these fundamental rights to the benefit of the State at the expense of common people. Article 22 provides protection against arbitrary arrest and detention, and it states that any arrested citizens should be brought before the nearest magistrate within twenty-four hours. However, in clauses (3) to (7), it provides for exceptions which allow Parliament to make laws that allow the State to arrest and detain anyone for as long as it wants, without even informing the detainee of the grounds on which he or she was arrested.

22. **(1)** No person who is arrested shall be detained in custody without being informed, as soon as may be, of the grounds for such arrest nor shall he be denied the right to consult, and to be defended by, a legal practitioner of his choice.

(2) Every person who is arrested and detained in custody shall be produced before the nearest magistrate within a period of twenty-four hours of such arrest excluding the time necessary for the journey from the place of arrest to the court of the magistrate and no such person shall be detained in custody beyond the said period without the authority of a magistrate.

(3) Nothing in clauses (1) and (2) shall apply—

(a) to any person who for the time being is an enemy alien; or

(b) to any person who is arrested or detained under any law providing for preventive detention.

(4) No law providing for preventive detention shall authorise the detention of a person for a longer period than three months unless—

(a) an Advisory Board consisting of persons who are, or have been, or are qualified to be appointed as, Judges of a High Court has reported before the expiration of the said period of three months that there is in its opinion sufficient cause for such detention:

(b) such person is detained in accordance with the provisions of any law made by Parliament under sub-clauses (a) and (b) of clause (7).

(5) When any person is detained in pursuance of an order made under any law providing for preventive detention, the authority making the order shall, as soon as may be, communicate to such person the grounds on which the order has been made and shall afford him the earliest opportunity of making a representation against the order.

(6) Nothing in clause (5) shall require the authority making any such order as is referred to in that clause to disclose facts which such authority considers to be against the public interest to disclose.

(7) Parliament may by law prescribe—

(a) the circumstances under which, and the class or classes of cases in which, a person may be detained for a period longer than three months under any law providing for preventive detention without obtaining the opinion of an Advisory Board in accordance with the provisions of sub-clause (a) of clause (4);

(b) the maximum period for which any person may in any class or classes of cases be detained under any law providing for preventive detention; and

(c) the procedure to be followed by an Advisory Board in an inquiry under sub-clause (a) of clause (4).

The lack of a safety valve for citizens is also clear in Article 31C, which says that the rights Article 14 or Article 19 grant shall not constrain the State from making any law that has been declared to be in pursuance of the principles in Part IV, which make up the Directive Principles of State Policy. What is strange is that once a law has been declared to be in pursuance of said goals, it cannot be challenged in court on the basis that it is not in pursuance of them. In other words, the State can declare any law to be in pursuance of these principles, and neither any article in Part III nor any court can restrain it.

> **31C.** Notwithstanding anything contained in article 13, no law giving effect to the policy of the State towards securing all or any of the principles laid down in Part IV shall be deemed to be void on the ground that it is inconsistent with, or takes away or abridges any of the rights conferred by article 14 or article 19; *and no law containing a declaration that it is for giving effect to such policy shall be called in question in any court on the ground that it does not give effect to such policy:*
>
> Provided that where such law is made by the Legislature of a State, the provisions of this article shall not apply thereto unless such law, having been reserved for the consideration of the President, has received his assent.

One of the footnotes to Article 31C says:

> In Kesavananda Bharati vs. The State of Kerala, (1973) Supp. S.C.R. 1, the Supreme Court held the provision in italics to be invalid.

The narrative in italics that is being referred to is:

> *and no law containing a declaration that it is for giving effect to such policy shall be called in question in any court on the ground that it does not give effect to such policy.*

It is astonishing that though Supreme Court held this provision to be invalid in 1973, it remains a valid part of the Constitution even in 2018.

Similarly, in 1980, the Supreme Court declared another provision of the same Article (31C) to be invalid in *Minerva Mills Ltd. and Oth-*

ers vs. Union of India and Others. In spite of what the Supreme Court held, the questionable provision stands tall in the Constitution. One can conclude that the Supreme Court, like the people of India, is helpless to alter the contentious "fundamental rights" enshrined in the Constitution.

Another unusual feature of the Constitution is that it does not prohibit the practice of the caste system[4]. Article 17 seems to ban untouchability, but because it mentions the word in quotation marks, it does not define it or elaborate on what it really means.

Frankly, the people of India did not expect to see this Constitution in such slippery terms. When all is said and done, these people have no one in government structures of India to protect their human rights.

2

The Union

Now, Sir, we have inherited a tradition. People always keep on saying to me: "Oh, you are the maker of the Constitution." My answer is I was a hack. What I was asked to do, I did much against my will.

—B.R. Ambedkar
September 2, 1953, Rajya Sabha

In this chapter, we shall look at the working of the Union government (also called Government of India) and investigate whether there is any horizontal distribution of powers.

The Government

Article 12 makes a distinction between Government and Parliament, which means that "Government" refers not to the Legislature but to the Executive. The executive power of the Union is vested in the President.

12. In this Part, unless the context otherwise requires, "the State" includes the Government and Parliament of India and the Government and the Legislature of each of the States and all local or other authorities within the territory of India or under the control of the Government of India.

53. (1) The executive power of the Union shall be vested in the President and shall be exercised by him either directly or through officers subordinate to him in accordance with this Constitution.

(2) Without prejudice to the generality of the foregoing provision, the supreme command of the Defence Forces of the Union shall be vested in the President and the exercise thereof shall be regulated by law.

(3) Nothing in this article shall—

(a) be deemed to transfer to the President any functions conferred by any existing law on the Government of any State or other authority; or

(b) prevent Parliament from conferring by law functions on authorities other than the President.

The elected members of the two houses of the Parliament and the elected members of the various State Assemblies elect the President.

54. The President shall be elected by the members of an electoral college consisting of—

(a) the elected members of both Houses of Parliament; and

(b) the elected members of the Legislative Assemblies of the States.

Explanation.—In this article and in article 55, "State" includes the National Capital Territory of Delhi and the Union territory of Pondicherry.

The above narrative might mislead the reader to think the President heads the executive branch in India. However, Article 54 must be read in conjunction with Article 74, which states that the President shall act according to the advice of the Prime Minister. Thus, the Prime Minister of India is the real head of Government, while the President is the ceremonial head.

74. **(1)** There shall be a Council of Ministers with the Prime Minister at the head to aid and advise the President who shall, in the exercise of his functions, act in accordance with such advice:

Provided that the President may require the Council of Ministers to reconsider such advice, either generally or otherwise, and the President shall act in accordance with the advice tendered after such reconsideration.

(2) The question whether any, and if so what, advice was tendered by Ministers to the President shall not be inquired into in any court.

An unusual feature of this article is that Clause (2) forbids any inquiry into the advice the Prime Minister tenders to the President.

Article 75 states that the President appoints the Prime Minister. A striking feature of this article is that there is no requirement for the Prime Minister to be elected before assuming the office and its duties. The only requirement is that the person should be a member of either house of Parliament. But as we shall see next, the Rajya Sabha (the Upper House also known as the Council of States) of Parliament offers a backdoor entry whereby anyone can become a member without running a due election process.

75. **(1)** The Prime Minister shall be appointed by the President and the other Ministers shall be appointed by the President on the advice of the Prime Minister.

(1A) The total number of Ministers, including the Prime Minister, in the Council of Ministers shall not exceed fifteen per cent. of the total number of members of the House of the People.

(1B) A member of either House of Parliament belonging to any political party who is disqualified for being a member of that House under paragraph 2 of the Tenth Schedule shall also be disqualified to be appointed as a Minister under clause (1) for duration of the period commencing from the date of his disqualification till the date on which the term of his office as such member would expire or where he contests any election to either House of Parliament before the expiry of such period, till the date on which he is declared elected, whichever is earlier.

(2) The Ministers shall hold office during the pleasure of the President.

(3) The Council of Ministers shall be collectively responsible to the House of the People.

(4) Before a Minister enters upon his office, the President shall administer to him the oaths of office and of secrecy according to the forms set out for the purpose in the Third Schedule.

(5) A Minister who for any period of six consecutive months is not a member of either House of Parliament shall at the expiration of that period cease to be a Minister.

(6) The salaries and allowances of Ministers shall be such as Parliament may from time to time by law determine and, until Parliament so determines, shall be as specified in the Second Schedule.

Article 80 describes the appointment of the members of the Rajya Sabha (Council of States). The Legislative Assemblies of various States choose most of the Rajya Sabha members indirectly, but the

President can arbitrarily choose twelve of them.

80. (1) The Council of States shall consist of—

(a) twelve members to be nominated by the President in accordance with the provisions of clause (3); and

(b) not more than two hundred and thirty-eight representatives of the States and of the Union territories.

(2) The allocation of seats in the Council of States to be filled by representatives of the States and of the Union territories shall be in accordance with the provisions in that behalf contained in the Fourth Schedule.

(3) The members to be nominated by the President under sub-clause (a) of clause (1) shall consist of persons having special knowledge or practical experience in respect of such matters as the following, namely:—

Literature, science, art and social service.

(4) The representatives of each State in the Council of States shall be elected by the elected members of the Legislative Assembly of the State in accordance with the system of proportional representation by means of the single transferable vote.

(5) The representatives of the Union territories in the Council of States shall be chosen in such manner as Parliament may by law prescribe.

The Rajya Sabha is a backdoor entry into Parliament, thereby bypassing the regular election process where a candidate must compete against the opposition in an open public arena. For example, Dr. Manmohan Singh, who was India's Prime Minister from 2004 to 2014, had never run in an authentic election—and he happened to be one among other unelected prime ministers of India since 1947.

We are told that this Constitution is essentially a replica of the British parliamentary system. Then why do we have a President and Vice President? Also, if the President is only supposed to be a mere puppet of the Prime Minister, then why do we even need that office?

The Parliament

The Parliament of India consists of the President and two houses: Lok Sabha (House of the People) and Rajya Sabha.

79. There shall be a Parliament for the Union which shall consist of the President and two Houses to be known respectively as the Council of States and the House of the People.

The Lok Sabha currently has 545 seats, and according to Article 81, members who are chosen via direct election from territorial constituencies must occupy them.

81. (1) Subject to the provisions of article 331, the House of the People shall consist of—

(a) not more than five hundred and thirty members chosen by direct election from territorial constituencies in the States, and

(b) not more than twenty members to represent the Union territories, chosen in such manner as Parliament may by law provide.

(2) For the purposes of sub-clause (a) of clause (1),—

(a) there shall be allotted to each State a number of seats in the House of the People in such manner that the ratio between that number and the population of the State is, so far as practicable, the same for all States; and

(b) each State shall be divided into territorial constituencies in such manner that the ratio between the population of each constituency and the number of seats allotted to it is, so far as practicable, the same throughout the State:

Provided that the provisions of sub-clause (a) of this clause shall not be applicable for the purpose of allotment of seats in the House of the People to any State so long as the population of that State does not exceed six millions.

(3) In this article, the expression "population" means the

population as ascertained at the last preceding census of which the relevant figures have been published:

Provided that the reference in this clause to the last preceding census of which the relevant figures have been published shall, until the relevant figures for the first census taken after the year 2026 have been published, be construed,—

(i) for the purposes of sub-clause (a) of clause (2) and the proviso to that clause, as a reference to the 1971 census; and

(ii) for the purposes of sub-clause (b) of clause (2) as a reference to the 2001 census.

Article 100 provides that a majority of votes decides all matters in a session of Parliament. However, members of Parliament are not allowed to vote according to their discretion. Paragraph 2 of the **Tenth Schedule** of the Constitution provides that the members of a House of Legislature who do not vote according to the directions of party heads are disqualified from that House.

2. Disqualification on ground of defection.—(1) Subject to the provisions of paragraphs 4 and 5, a member of a House belonging to any political party shall be disqualified for being a member of the House—

(a) if he has voluntarily given up his membership of such political party; or

(b) if he votes or abstains from voting in such House contrary to any direction issued by the political party to which he belongs or by any person or authority authorised by it in this behalf, without obtaining, in either case, the prior permission of such political party, person or authority and such voting or abstention has not been condoned by such political party, person or authority within fifteen days from the date of such voting or abstention.

Explanation.—For the purposes of this sub-paragraph,—

(a) an elected member of a House shall be deemed to belong to the political party, if any, by which he was set up as a candidate for election as such member;

(b) a nominated member of a House shall,—

(i) where he is a member of any political party on the date of his nomination as such member, be deemed to belong to such political party;

(ii) in any other case, be deemed to belong to the political party of which he becomes, or, as the case may be, first becomes, a member before the expiry of six months from the date on which he takes his seat after complying with the requirements of article 99 or, as the case may be, article 188.

(2) An elected member of a House who has been elected as such otherwise than as a candidate set up by any political party shall be disqualified for being a member of the House if he joins any political party after such election.

(3) A nominated member of a House shall be disqualified for being a member of the House if he joins any political party after the expiry of six months from the date on which he takes his seat after complying with the requirements of article 99 or, as the case may be, article 188.

(4) Notwithstanding anything contained in the foregoing provisions of this paragraph, a person who, on the commencement of the Constitution (Fifty-second Amendment) Act, 1985, is a member of a House (whether elected or nominated as such) shall,—

(i) where he was a member of political party immediately before such commencement, be deemed, for the purposes of sub-paragraph (1) of this paragraph, to have been elected as a member of such House as a candidate set up by such political party;

(ii) in any other case, be deemed to be an elected member of the House who has been elected as such otherwise than as a candidate set up by any political party for the purposes of sub-paragraph (2) of this paragraph or, as the case may be, be deemed to be a nominated member of the House for the purposes of sub-paragraph (3) of this paragraph.

According to the foregoing provision, any Member of Parliament (MP) who votes (or abstains from voting) against the will of the party boss is expelled from Parliament. This control mechanism calls into question the purpose of electing an MP. Alternatively, what is the purpose of ritually staging an election season every five years[5]?

Another issue of concern is Article 117, which provides that a Bill which would involve the expenditure of money on its enactment cannot even be introduced in a House without the recommendation of the President.

117. (1) A Bill or amendment making provision for any of the matters specified in sub-clauses (a) to (f) of clause (1) of article 110 shall not be introduced or moved except on the recommendation of the President and a Bill making such provision shall not be introduced in the Council of States:

Provided that no recommendation shall be required under this clause for the moving of an amendment making provision for the reduction or abolition of any tax.

(2) A Bill or amendment shall not be deemed to make provision for any of the matters aforesaid by reason only that it provides for the imposition of fines or other pecuniary penalties, or for the demand or payment of fees for licences or fees for services rendered, or by reason that it provides for the imposition, abolition, remission, alteration or regulation of any tax by any local authority or body for local purposes.

(3) A Bill which, if enacted and brought into operation, would involve expenditure from the Consolidated Fund of India shall not be passed by either House of Parliament unless the President has recommended to that House the consideration of the Bill.

Because most public policy issues involve the expenditure of money, they are rendered beyond the prerogative of MPs. Only the executive (using the President) can introduce such bills. MPs can move irrelevant or minor issues which do not involve money, such as some resolutions or honors.

A disturbing feature of the Constitution is that the Prime Minister (using the President) can prorogue or dissolve the Parliament without explanation. The provision for this is contained in Article 85.

85. (1) The President shall from time to time summon each House of Parliament to meet at such time and place as he thinks fit, but six months shall not intervene between its last sitting in one session and the date appointed for its first sitting in the next session.

(2) The President may from time to time—

(a) prorogue the Houses or either House;

(b) dissolve the House of the People.

For the foregoing reasons, the lawmaking power of Parliament is limited and controlled by the executive as well as the party bosses.

The Judiciary

To understand the status of the judiciary in India, we need to take a close look at the Directive Principles of State Policy that form Part IV of the Constitution. In this Part, "State" has the same meaning as it does in Article 12.

36. In this Part, unless the context otherwise requires, "the State" has the same meaning as in Part III.

Article 50 provides that the State shall endeavor to separate the judiciary from the executive.

50. The State shall take steps to separate the judiciary from the executive in the public services of the State.

However, Article 37 provides that the provisions contained in the Directive Principles (Part IV) are not binding on the Government.

37. The provisions contained in this Part shall not be enforceable by any court, but the principles therein laid down are nevertheless fundamental in the governance of the country and it shall be the duty of the State to apply these principles in making laws.

In other words, there is no constitutional requirement for the separation and independence of the judiciary from the executive.

3

The States

Sir, my friends tell me that I have made the constitution. But I am quite prepared to say that I shall be the first person to burn it out. I do not want it. It does not suit anybody.

—B.R. Ambedkar
September 2, 1953, Rajya Sabha

A State is a territorial unit of the Union of India. The States that make up the Union of India are listed in the **First Schedule**. Currently, there are twenty-nine States in India. Every few years, the citizens of these States go through the rigors of elections. In this chapter, we shall consider whether these elections serve any useful purpose.

The Government

The definition of "Government" in Article 12 also applies to States. The executive power of the State is vested in the Governor, and hence the "Government of a State" refers to the Governor of that State.

154. (1) The executive power of the State shall be vested in the Governor and shall be exercised by him either directly or through officers subordinate to him in accordance with this Constitution.

(2) Nothing in this article shall—

(a) be deemed to transfer to the Governor any functions conferred by any existing law on any other authority; or

(b) prevent Parliament or the Legislature of the State from conferring by law functions on any authority subordinate to the Governor.

The Governor is appointed by the President, whom the Prime Minister and Cabinet control. Because the President can impeach a Governor at will, the Governor is really responsible to no one but the Union Executive.

155. The Governor of a State shall be appointed by the President by warrant under his hand and seal.

156. (1) The Governor shall hold office during the pleasure of the President.

(2) The Governor may, by writing under his hand addressed to the President, resign his office.

(3) Subject to the foregoing provisions of this article, a Governor shall hold office for a term of five years from the date on which he enters upon his office:

Provided that a Governor shall, notwithstanding the expiration of his term, continue to hold office until his successor enters upon his office.

A common misconception among Indians is how they perceive the relationship between the Governor and Chief Minister. Indians often draw an analogy between the State and Union. Because the Prime Minister is the real head while the President is a ceremonial chief at the Union level, Indians assume that the Chief Minister is the real head while the Governor is the ceremonial chief at the State level too. However, Article 163 challenges this assumption. We have reproduced both Article 74 (which deals with the Union) and Article 163 (which deals with the State) below for the reader to go through before we analyze them.

74. (1) There shall be a Council of Ministers with the Prime Minister at the head to aid and advise the President who shall, in the exercise of his functions, act in accordance with such advice:

Provided that the President may require the Council of Ministers to reconsider such advice, either generally or otherwise, and the President shall act in accordance with the advice tendered after such reconsideration.

(2) The question whether any, and if so what, advice was tendered by Ministers to the President shall not be inquired into in any court.

163. (1) There shall be a Council of Ministers with the Chief Minister at the head to aid and advise the Governor in the exercise of his functions, except in so far as he is by or under this Constitution required to exercise his functions or any of them in his discretion.

(2) If any question arises whether any matter is or is not a matter as respects which the Governor is by or under this Constitution required to act in his discretion, the decision

of the Governor in his discretion shall be final, and the validity of anything done by the Governor shall not be called in question on the ground that he ought or ought not to have acted in his discretion.

(3) The question whether any, and if so what, advice was tendered by Ministers to the Governor shall not be inquired into in any court.

The contrast between the two articles is stark. First, Article 163 does not require the Governor to act according to the advice of the Council of Ministers, whereas Article 74 makes it explicit that the President "shall" act according to the advice of said Council. Second, there is no exception in Article 74, whereas Article 163 allows the Governor to act in his or her discretion in certain matters. Finally, Article 163 uniquely states that in case of a dispute, the decision of the Governor is final and not subject to challenge or question. Based on the foregoing provisions, the Governor is the real executive head of State, and the Chief Minister is merely an advisor.

Article 164 states that the Governor appoints the Chief Minister. As is the case with the Prime Minister, there is no requirement for the Chief Minister to be elected. The only requirement is that the person should be a member of either house of the State Legislature.

164. (1) The Chief Minister shall be appointed by the Governor and the other Ministers shall be appointed by the Governor on the advice of the Chief Minister, and the Ministers shall hold office during the pleasure of the Governor:

Provided that in the States of Chhattisgarh, Jharkhand, Madhya Pradesh and Odisha there shall be a Minister in charge of tribal welfare who may in addition be in charge of the welfare of the Scheduled Castes and backward classes or any other work.

(1A) The total number of Ministers, including the Chief Minister, in the Council of Ministers in a State shall not exceed fifteen per cent. of the total number of members of the Legislative Assembly of that State:

Provided that the number of Ministers, including the Chief Minister in a State shall not be less than twelve:

Provided further that where the total number of Ministers including the Chief Minister in the Council of Ministers in any State at the commencement of the Constitution (Ninety-first Amendment) Act, 2003 exceeds the said fifteen per cent. or the number specified in the first proviso, as the case may be, then the total number of Ministers in that State shall be brought in conformity with the provisions of this clause within six months from such date as the President may by public notification appoint.

(1B) A member of the Legislative Assembly of a State or either House of the Legislature of a State having Legislative Council belonging to any political party who is disqualified for being a member of that House under paragraph 2 of the Tenth Schedule shall also be disqualified to be appointed as a Minister under clause (1) for duration of the period commencing from the date of his disqualification till the date on which the term of his office as such member would expire or where he contests any election to the Legislative Assembly of a State or either House of the Legislature of a State having Legislative Council, as the case may be, before the expiry of such period, till the date on which he is declared elected, whichever is earlier.

(2) The Council of Ministers shall be collectively responsible to the Legislative Assembly of the State.

(3) Before a Minister enters upon his office, the Governor shall administer to him the oaths of office and of secrecy according to the forms set out for the purpose in the Third Schedule.

(4) A Minister who for any period of six consecutive months is not a member of the Legislature of the State shall at the expiration of that period cease to be a Minister.

(5) The salaries and allowances of Ministers shall be such as the Legislature of the State may from time to time by law determine and, until the Legislature of the State so

determines, shall be as specified in the Second Schedule

The appointment of the members of the Legislative Council is described in Article 171. Most of the members are elected through one or the other procedure, but others—up to one-sixth of the total members—could be arbitrarily appointed by the Governor.

171. (1) The total number of members in the Legislative Council of a State having such a Council shall not exceed one-third of the total number of members in the Legislative Assembly of that State:

Provided that the total number of members in the Legislative Council of a State shall in no case be less than forty.

(2) Until Parliament by law otherwise provides, the composition of the Legislative Council of a State shall be as provided in clause (3).

(3) Of the total number of members of the Legislative Council of a State—

(a) as nearly as may be, one-third shall be elected by electorates consisting of members of municipalities, district boards and such other local authorities in the State as Parliament may by law specify;

(b) as nearly as may be, one-twelfth shall be elected by electorates consisting of persons residing in the State who have been for at least three years graduates of any university in the territory of India or have been for at least three years in possession of qualifications prescribed by or under any law made by Parliament as equivalent to that of a graduate of any such university;

(c) as nearly as may be, one-twelfth shall be elected by electorates consisting of persons who have been for at least three years engaged in teaching in such educational institutions within the State, not lower in standard than that of a secondary school, as may be prescribed by or under any law made by Parliament;

(d) as nearly as may be, one-third shall be elected by

the members of the Legislative Assembly of the State from amongst persons who are not members of the Assembly;

(e) the remainder shall be nominated by the Governor in accordance with the provisions of clause (5).

(4) The members to be elected under sub-clauses (a), (b) and (c) of clause (3) shall be chosen in such territorial constituencies as may be prescribed by or under any law made by Parliament, and the elections under the said sub-clauses and under sub-clause (d) of the said clause shall be held in accordance with the system of proportional representation by means of the single transferable vote

(5) The members to be nominated by the Governor under sub-clause (e) of clause (3) shall consist of persons having special knowledge or practical experience in respect of such matters as the following, namely:—

Literature, science, art, co-operative movement and social service.

Again, as is with the case at the Union, the upper house of the State Legislature (for States that have two houses) provides a backdoor entry. The most recent example of exploitation of this form of entry is Yogi Adityanath (Ajay Mohan Bisht), who never sought any election in his State for purposes of seeking entry into its legislature, and yet as of this writing is the Chief Minister of Uttar Pradesh, the most populous State in India.

The Legislature

The State Legislature consists of the Governor and one House in most States or two in others. The lower house of a State Legislature is called the Legislative Assembly. The upper house (in States that have two houses) is called the Legislative Council.

However, what is unusual about this setup is that the Governor—who is the head of the executive of the State—is also a "permanent" but unelected member of the State Legislature.

168. (1) For every State there shall be a Legislature which shall consist of the Governor, and—

(a) in the States of Andhra Pradesh, Bihar, Madhya Pradesh, Maharashtra, Karnataka, Tamil Nadu, Telangana and Uttar Pradesh, two Houses;

(b) in other States, one House.

(2) Where there are two Houses of the Legislature of a State, one shall be known as the Legislative Council and the other as the Legislative Assembly, and where there is only one House, it shall be known as the Legislative Assembly.

According to Article 170, the members of the Legislative Assembly are chosen by direct elections.

170. (1) Subject to the provisions of article 333, the Legislative Assembly of each State shall consist of not more than five hundred, and not less than sixty, members chosen by direct election from territorial constituencies in the State.

(2) For the purposes of clause (1), each State shall be divided into territorial constituencies in such manner that the ratio between the population of each constituency and the number of seats allotted to it shall, so far as practicable, be the same throughout the State

Explanation.—In this clause, the expression "population" means the population as ascertained at the last preceding census of which the relevant figures have been published:

Provided that the reference in this Explanation to the last preceding census of which the relevant figures have been published shall, until the relevant figures for the first census taken after the year 2026 have been published, be construed as a reference to the 2001 census.

(3) Upon the completion of each census, the total number of seats in the Legislative Assembly of each State and the division of each State into territorial constituencies

shall be readjusted by such authority and in such manner as Parliament may by law determine

Provided that such readjustment shall not affect representation in the Legislative Assembly until the dissolution of the then existing Assembly:

Provided further that such readjustment shall take effect from such date as the President may, by order, specify and until such readjustment takes effect, any election to the Legislative Assembly may be held on the basis of the territorial constituencies existing before such readjustment:

Provided also that until the relevant figures for the first census taken after the year 2026 have been published, it shall not be necessary to readjust—

(i) the total number of seats in the Legislative Assembly of each State as readjusted on the basis of the 1971 census; and

(ii) the division of such State into territorial constituencies as may be readjusted on the basis of the 2001 census, under this clause.

All matters in the State Assembly are decided by direct vote, but as is the case at the Union, the members of the Legislature of the State[6] do not have a right to vote freely. The provisions for disqualification on grounds of defection contained in the second paragraph of the **Tenth Schedule** also apply to the members of State Legislature.

In addition, Article 207 provides that any bill that involves the expenditure of money from the Consolidated Fund of the State cannot be introduced except on the recommendation of the Governor.

207. (1) A Bill or amendment making provision for any of the matters specified in sub-clauses (a) to (f) of clause (1) of article 199 shall not be introduced or moved except on the recommendation of the Governor, and a Bill making such provision shall not be introduced in a Legislative Council

Provided that no recommendation shall be required under this clause for the moving of an amendment making provision for the reduction or abolition of any tax.

(2) A Bill or amendment shall not be deemed to make provision for any of the matters aforesaid by reason only that it provides for the imposition of fines or other pecuniary penalties, or for the demand or payment of fees for licences or fees for services rendered, or by reason that it provides for the imposition, abolition, remission, alteration or regulation of any tax by any local authority or body for local purposes.

(3) A Bill which, if enacted and brought into operation, would involve expenditure from the Consolidated Fund of a State shall not be passed by a House of the Legislature of the State unless the Governor has recommended to that House the consideration of the Bill.

The above article is bewildering because the Legislative Assembly, elected by the people of the State, cannot spend any money from the Consolidated Fund of its own State without permission from the unelected Governor.

In addition, articles 200 and 201 provide that any bill the State Legislature passes must be assented to by the Governor before it can become law. Based on these Articles, the Governor has the following options when the State Assembly passes a bill:

1. Assent to the Bill

2. Withhold assent

3. Reserve the Bill for the consideration of the President

4. If the Bill is not a Money Bill, send it back to State Assemblies for reconsideration.

If the Governor chooses option 4, he should do it "as soon as possible after the presentation to him of the Bill," but for the first three options, there is no time limit.[7]

200. When a Bill has been passed by the Legislative Assembly of a State or, in the case of a State having a Legislative Council, has been passed by both Houses of the

Legislature of the State, it shall be presented to the Governor and the Governor shall declare either that he assents to the Bill or that he withholds assent therefrom or that he reserves the Bill for the consideration of the President:

Provided that the Governor may, as soon as possible after the presentation to him of the Bill for assent, return the Bill if it is not a Money Bill together with a message requesting that the House or Houses will reconsider the Bill or any specified provisions thereof and, in particular, will consider the desirability of introducing any such amendments as he may recommend in his message and, when a Bill is so returned, the House or Houses shall reconsider the Bill accordingly, and if the Bill is passed again by the House or Houses with or without amendment and presented to the Governor for assent, the Governor shall not withhold assent therefrom:

Provided further that the Governor shall not assent to, but shall reserve for the consideration of the President, any Bill which in the opinion of the Governor would, if it became law, so derogate from the powers of the High Court as to endanger the position which that Court is by this Constitution designed to fill.

201. When a Bill is reserved by a Governor for the consideration of the President, the President shall declare either that he assents to the Bill or that he withholds assent therefrom:

Provided that, where the Bill is not a Money Bill, the President may direct the Governor to return the Bill to the House or, as the case may be, the Houses of the Legislature of the State together with such a message as is mentioned in the first proviso to article 200 and, when a Bill is so returned, the House or Houses shall reconsider it accordingly within a period of six months from the date of receipt of such message and, if it is again passed by the House or Houses with or without amendment, it shall be presented again to the President for his consideration.

We have already seen that there can be no Money Bill without the recommendation of the Governor, but according to the foregoing provisions, even ordinary bills passed by the State Assembly may not become law if the Governor so desires.

Let us provide another example which shows how powerless the State Assembly is. First, the reader should know the concept of the vertical (between the Union and States) division of power in the Indian Constitution. The **Seventh Schedule** specifies three Lists for that purpose: (1) the Union List, which contains the areas under the legislative and executive power of the Union; (2) the Concurrent List, which contains the areas under the power of both the Union and State (with the Union overriding the State); and (3) the State List, which contains the areas under the exclusive legislative and executive power of the State.

However, Article 258A provides that it is clear that the unelected Governor—with the consent of the Government of India—can "entrust" any function belonging to the State's executive power directly to the Union. Only the consent of Union Executive is required, while no consent is needed from the State Legislative Assembly

> **258A.** Notwithstanding anything in this Constitution, the Governor of a State may, with the consent of the Government of India, entrust either conditionally or unconditionally to that Government or to its officers functions in relation to any matter to which the executive power of the State extends.

We can conclude that all executive and legislative power in a State is vested in the Union Executive and exercised through the unelected Governor. Therefore, we can address the issue raised earlier: what is the purpose of conducting elections in the State? There is no purpose within the dictates of an absent "valid democracy" in India.[8] In addition to the fact of impotent State Legislative Assemblies, the Union government can arbitrarily impose direct President's rule over a State.[9]

4

The Union Territories

There is great danger of things going wrong. Times are fast changing. People including our own are being moved by new ideologies. They are getting tired of Government by the people. They are prepared to have Governments for the people and are indifferent whether it is Government of the people and by the people. If we wish to preserve the Constitution in which we have sought to enshrine the principle of Government of the people, for the people and by the people, let us resolve not to be tardy in the recognition of the evils that lie across our path and which induce people to prefer Government for the people to Government by the people, nor to be weak in our initiative to remove them. That is the only way to serve the country. I know of no better.

—B.R. Ambedkar
Constituent Assembly Debates
Vol. XI, November 25, 1949

A Union territory (UT) is a territorial unit that is smaller than the State. There are seven UTs in India: the Andaman and Nicobar Islands, Lakshadweep, Dadra and Nagar Haveli, Daman and Diu, Puducherry, Chandigarh, and the National Capital Territory of Delhi.

According to Article 239, the Union government administers the UTs directly.

239. (1) Save as otherwise provided by Parliament by law, every Union territory shall be administered by the President acting, to such extent as he thinks fit, through an administrator to be appointed by him with such designation as he may specify.

(2) Notwithstanding anything contained in Part VI, the President may appoint the Governor of a State as the administrator of an adjoining Union territory, and where a Governor is so appointed, he shall exercise his functions as such administrator independently of his Council of Ministers.

However, Article 239AA makes an exception for the UT of Delhi, which is also called the National Capital Territory. It provides for the existence of a Legislative Assembly for the National Capital Territory whose members are chosen by direct elections. However, clauses (3) and (4) provide that an unelected official appointed by the Union—the Lieutenant Governor—wields all the executive and legislative powers.

239AA. (1) As from the date of commencement of the Constitution (Sixty-ninth Amendment) Act, 1991, the Union territory of Delhi shall be called the National Capital Territory of Delhi (hereafter in this Part referred to as the National Capital Territory) and the administrator thereof appointed under article 239 shall be designated as the Lieutenant Governor.

(2) (a) There shall be a Legislative Assembly for the National Capital Territory and the seats in such Assembly shall be filled by members chosen by direct election from territorial constituencies in the National Capital Territory.

(b) The total number of seats in the Legislative Assembly, the number of seats reserved for Scheduled Castes, the division of the National Capital Territory into territorial constituencies (including the basis for such division) and all other matters relating to the functioning of the Legislative Assembly shall be regulated by law made by Parliament.

(c) The provisions of articles 324 to 327 and 329 shall apply in relation to the National Capital Territory, the Legislative Assembly of the National Capital Territory and the members thereof as they apply, in relation to a State, the Legislative Assembly of a State and the members thereof respectively; and any reference in articles 326 and 329 to "appropriate Legislature" shall be deemed to be a reference to Parliament.

(3) (a) Subject to the provisions of this Constitution, the Legislative Assembly shall have power to make laws for the whole or any part of the National Capital Territory with respect to any of the matters enumerated in the State List or in the Concurrent List in so far as any such matter is applicable to Union territories except matters with respect to Entries 1, 2 and 18 of the State List and Entries 64, 65 and 66 of that List in so far as they relate to the said Entries 1, 2 and 18.

(b) Nothing in sub-clause (a) shall derogate from the powers of Parliament under this Constitution to make laws with respect to any matter for a Union territory or any part thereof.

(c) If any provision of a law made by the Legislative Assembly with respect to any matter is repugnant to any provision of a law made by Parliament with respect to that matter, whether passed before or after the law made by the Legislative Assembly, or of an earlier law, other than a law made by the Legislative Assembly, then, in either case, the law made by Parliament, or, as the case may be, such earlier law, shall prevail and the law made by the Legislative Assembly shall, to the extent of the repugnancy, be void:

Provided that if any such law made by the Legislative Assembly has been reserved for the consideration of the President and has received his assent, such law shall prevail in the National Capital Territory:

Provided further that nothing in this sub-clause shall prevent Parliament from enacting at any time any law with respect to the same matter including a law adding to, amending, varying or repealing the law so made by the Legislative Assembly.

(4) There shall be a Council of Ministers consisting of not more than ten per cent. of the total number of members in the Legislative Assembly, with the Chief Minister at the head to aid and advise the Lieutenant Governor in the exercise of his functions in relation to matters with respect to which the Legislative Assembly has power to make laws, except in so far as he is, by or under any law, required to act in his discretion:

Provided that in the case of difference of opinion between the Lieutenant Governor and his Ministers on any matter, the Lieutenant Governor shall refer it to the President for decision and act according to the decision given thereon by the President and pending such decision it shall be competent for the Lieutenant Governor in any case where the matter, in his opinion, is so urgent that it is necessary for him to take immediate action, to take such action or to give such direction in the matter as he deems necessary.

(5) The Chief Minister shall be appointed by the President and the other Ministers shall be appointed by the President on the advice of the Chief Minister and the Ministers shall hold office during the pleasure of the President.

(6) The Council of Ministers shall be collectively responsible to the Legislative Assembly.

(7) (a) Parliament may, by law, make provisions for giving effect to, or supplementing the provisions contained in the foregoing clauses and for all matters incidental or consequential thereto.

(b) Any such law as is referred to in sub-clause (a) shall not be deemed to be an amendment of this Constitution for the purposes of article 368 notwithstanding that it contains any provision which amends or has the effect of amending, this Constitution.

(8) The provisions of article 239B shall, so far as may be, apply in relation to the National Capital Territory, the Lieutenant Governor and the Legislative Assembly, as they apply in relation to the Union territory of Puducherry, the administrator and its Legislature, respectively; and any reference in that article to "clause (1) of article 239A" shall be deemed to be a reference to this article or article 239AB, as the case may be.

Again, we can conclude that there is no good purpose of conducting elections in the National Capital Territory. Like the example explored earlier at the State level, the chief executive appointee at the National Capital Territory remains unelected and therefore he/she answers only to those who had appointed this person to the position—in this case is the Union Executive headed by the Prime Minister. Do the regularly scheduled elections serve any purpose?

5

Emergency Provisions

The second charge is that the Centre [Government of India] has been given the power to override the States. This charge must be admitted. But before condemning the Constitution for containing such overriding powers, certain considerations must be borne in mind. The first is that these overriding powers do not form the normal feature of the constitution. Their use and operation are expressly confined to emergencies only. The second consideration is: Could we avoid giving overriding powers to the Centre when an emergency has arisen? Those who do not admit the justification for such overriding powers to the Centre even in an emergency, do not seem to have a clear idea of the problem which lies at the root of the matter.

—B.R. Ambedkar
Constituent Assembly Debates
Vol XI, November 25, 1949

The Emergency Provisions enshrined in the Indian Constitution are the cause of much controversy. There are no objective requirements for the declaration of such an emergency, and the degree of power it concentrates in the Union Executive is alarming. In this chapter, we will show you how easy it is for the Union government to use this Emergency Provisions to consolidate power at the expense of common citizens.

According to the Explanation in Clause (1) and Clause (9) of Article 352, even a mere perception of "imminent danger of war or external aggression or armed rebellion" allows the Union government to declare an emergency.

352. (1) If the President is satisfied that a grave emergency exists whereby the security of India or of any part of the territory thereof is threatened, whether by war or external aggression or armed rebellion, he may, by Proclamation, make a declaration to that effect in respect of the whole of India or of such part of the territory thereof as may be specified in the Proclamation.

Explanation.—A Proclamation of Emergency declaring that the security of India or any part of the territory thereof is threatened by war or by external aggression or by armed rebellion may be made before the actual occurrence of war or of any such aggression or rebellion, if the President is satisfied that there is imminent danger thereof.

(2) A Proclamation issued under clause (1) may be varied or revoked by a subsequent Proclamation.

(3) The President shall not issue a Proclamation under clause (1) or a Proclamation varying such Proclamation unless the decision of the Union Cabinet (that is to say, the Council consisting of the Prime Minister and other Ministers of Cabinet rank appointed under article 75) that such a Proclamation may be issued has been communicated to him in writing.

(4) Every Proclamation issued under this article shall be laid before each House of Parliament and shall, except

where it is a Proclamation revoking a previous Proclamation, cease to operate at the expiration of one month unless before the expiration of that period it has been approved by resolution of both Houses of Parliament:

Provided that if any such Proclamation (not being a Proclamation revoking a previous Proclamation) is issued at a time when the House of the People has been dissolved, or the dissolution of the House of the People takes place during the period of one month referred to in this clause, and if a resolution approving the Proclamation has been passed by the Council of States, but no resolution with respect to such Proclamation has been passed by the House of the People before the expiration of that period, the Proclamation shall cease to operate at the expiration of thirty days from the date on which the House of the People first sits after its reconstitution, unless before the expiration of the said period of thirty days a resolution approving the Proclamation has been also passed by the House of the People.

(5) A Proclamation so approved shall, unless revoked, cease to operate on the expiration of a period of six months from the date of the passing of the second of the resolutions approving the Proclamation under clause (4):

Provided that if and so often as a resolution approving the continuance in force of such a Proclamation is passed by both Houses of Parliament the Proclamation shall, unless revoked, continue in force for a further period of six months from the date on which it would otherwise have ceased to operate under this clause:

Provided further that if the dissolution of the House of the People takes place during any such period of six months and a resolution approving the continuance in force of such Proclamation has been passed by the Council of States but no resolution with respect to the continuance in force of such Proclamation has been pas-sed by the House of the People during the said period, the Proclamation shall cease to operate at the expiration of thirty days from the date on which the House of the People first sits after its reconstitution unless before the expiration of the said period of thirty days, a resolution approving the continuance in force of the Proclamation has been also passed by the House of the People.

(6) For the purposes of clauses (4) and (5), a resolution may be passed by either House of Parliament only by a majority of the total membership of that House and by a majority of not less than two-thirds of the members of that House present and voting.

(7) Notwithstanding anything contained in the foregoing clauses, the President shall revoke a Proclamation issued under clause (1) or a Proclamation varying such Proclamation if the House of the People passes a resolution disapproving, or, as the case may be, disapproving the continuance in force of, such Proclamation.

(8) Where a notice in writing signed by not less than one-tenth of the total number of members of the House of the People has been given, of their intention to move a resolution for disapproving, or, as the case may be, for disapproving the continuance in force of, a Proclamation issued under clause (1) or a Proclamation varying such Proclamation,—

(a) to the Speaker, if the House is in session; or

(b) to the President, if the House is not in session,

a special sitting of the House shall be held within fourteen days from the date on which such notice is received by the Speaker, or, as the case may be, by the President, for the purpose of considering such resolution.

(9) The power conferred on the President by this article shall include the power to issue different Proclamations on different grounds, being war or external aggression or armed rebellion or imminent danger of war or external aggression or armed rebellion, whether or not there is a

Proclamation already issued by the President under clause
(1) and such Proclamation is in operation.

According to Article 353, when an emergency has been declared,
the executive power of the Union shall extend to any State(s), including those not among the list of States where the said emergency was
initially declared. This is tantamount to saying that if an emergency
has been declared in any one part of India, the Union government—
which really is the Prime Minister and Cabinet—is vested with all executive power in India.

353. While a Proclamation of Emergency is in operation, then—

(a) notwithstanding anything in this Constitution, the
executive power of the Union shall extend to the giving
of directions to any State as to the manner in which the
executive power thereof is to be exercised;

(b) the power of Parliament to make laws with respect
to any matter shall include power to make laws conferring powers and imposing duties, or authorising the
conferring of powers and the imposition of duties, upon
the Union or officers and authorities of the Union as respects that matter, notwithstanding that it is one which
is not enumerated in the Union List:

Provided that where a Proclamation of Emergency is
in operation only in any part of the territory of India,—

(i) the executive power of the Union to give directions under clause (a), and

(ii) the power of Parliament to make laws under
clause (b),

shall also extend to any State other than a State in which
or in any part of which the Proclamation of Emergency is
in operation if and in so far as the security of India or any
part of the territory thereof is threatened by activities in
or in relation to the part of the territory of India in which
the Proclamation of Emergency is in operation.

According to Article 358, when an emergency is declared in one part of India, the "freedoms" bestowed in Article 19—which is devoid of freedoms to begin with as discussed in Chapter 1—are suspended and there are no limits on the executive power of the Union. This makes a mockery of fundamental rights.

358. **(1)** While a Proclamation of Emergency declaring that the security of India or any part of the territory thereof is threatened by war or by external aggression is in operation, nothing in article 19 shall restrict the power of the State as defined in Part III to make any law or to take any executive action which the State would but for the provisions contained in that Part be competent to make or to take, but any law so made shall, to the extent of the incompetency, cease to have effect as soon as the Proclamation ceases to operate, except as respects things done or omitted to be done before the law so ceases to have effect:

Provided that where such Proclamation of Emergency is in operation only in any part of the territory of India, any such law may be made, or any such executive action may be taken, under this article in relation to or in any State or Union territory in which or in any part of which the Proclamation of Emergency is not in operation, if and in so far as the security of India or any part of the territory thereof is threatened by activities in or in relation to the part of the territory of India in which the Proclamation of Emergency is in operation.

(2) Nothing in clause (1) shall apply—

(a) to any law which does not contain a recital to the effect that such law is in relation to the Proclamation of Emergency in operation when it is made; or

(b) to any executive action taken otherwise than under a law containing such a recital.

According to Article 359, when an emergency has been declared, the President may suspend the nationwide venue for approaching courts for the enforcement of the rights mentioned in Part III of the

Constitution.

359. **(1)** Where a Proclamation of Emergency is in operation, the President may by order declare that the right to move any court for the enforcement of such of the rights conferred by Part III (except articles 20 and 21) as may be mentioned in the order and all proceedings pending in any court for the enforcement of the rights so mentioned shall remain suspended for the period during which the Proclamation is in force or for such shorter period as may be specified in the order.

(1A) While an order made under clause (1) mentioning any of the rights conferred by Part III (except articles 20 and 21) is in operation, nothing in that Part conferring those rights shall restrict the power of the State as defined in the said Part to make any law or to take any executive action which the State would but for the provisions contained in that Part be competent to make or to take, but any law so made shall, to the extent of the incompetency, cease to have effect as soon as the order aforesaid ceases to operate, except as respects things done or omitted to be done before the law so ceases to have effect:

Provided that where a Proclamation of Emergency is in operation only in any part of the territory of India, any such law may be made, or any such executive action may be taken, under this article in relation to or in any State or Union territory in which or in any part of which the Proclamation of Emergency is not in operation, if and in so far as the security of India or any part of the territory thereof is threatened by activities in or in relation to the part of the territory of India in which the Proclamation of Emergency is in operation.

(1B) Nothing in clause (1A) shall apply—

(a) to any law which does not contain a recital to the effect that such law is in relation to the Proclamation of Emergency in operation when it is made; or

(b) to any executive action taken otherwise than under a law containing such a recital.

(2) An order made as aforesaid may extend to the whole or any part of the territory of India:

Provided that where a Proclamation of Emergency is in operation only in a part of the territory of India, any such order shall not extend to any other part of the territory of India unless the President, being satisfied that the security of India or any part of the territory thereof is threatened by activities in or in relation to the part of the territory of India in which the Proclamation of Emergency is in operation, considers such extension to be necessary.

(3) Every order made under clause (1) shall, as soon as may be after it is made, be laid before each House of Parliament

The above narrative again shows that there is no notion of fundamental rights in the Constitution. All rights allegedly given are provisional, subject to the interpretation of—and at the mercy of—those in power.

6

The Role of Modern Hinduism

The credit that is given to me does not really belong to me. It belongs partly to Sir B.N. Rau, the Constitutional Adviser to the Constituent Assembly who prepared a rough draft of the Constitution for the consideration of the Drafting Committee. A part of the credit must go to the members of the Drafting Committee who, as I have said, have sat for 141 days and without whose ingenuity of devise new formulae and capacity to tolerate and to accommodate different points of view, the task of framing the Constitution could not have come to so successful a conclusion. Much greater, share of the credit must go to Mr. S.N. Mukherjee, the Chief Draftsman of the Constitution. His ability to put the most intricate proposals in the simplest and clearest legal form can rarely be equalled, nor his capacity for hard work. He has been an acquisition to the Assembly. Without his help, this Assembly would have taken many more years to finalise the Constitution. I must not omit to mention the members of the staff working under Mr. Mukherjee. For, I know how hard they have worked and how long they have toiled sometimes even beyond midnight. I want to thank them all for their effort and their co-operation.

—B.R. Ambedkar
Constituent Assembly Debates
Vol. XI, November 25, 1949

The framework of Modern Hinduism is crucial to understand the Constitution because it provides deeper insights into the mystery surrounding this political document. What is Modern Hinduism?

With the introduction of British colonialism in the Bengal region of India, a new ideology was born that transformed classical and/or popular Hinduism. In other words, Modern Hinduism (also referred to as reformatory Hinduism or neo-Hinduism) is a reinterpretation of Hindu scriptures, ideas, or purported history based on the following nine competing, aggressive factors:

1. European colonialism

2. Christian missions

3. Western education and technology

4. Western means of propaganda and disinformation

5. Theosophy

6. Freemasonry

7. Nationalism

8. Communism and its varieties; and

9. Fascism

Over the years, various interpretations of Hinduism have arisen, starting with the Brahmo Samaj and its tributaries. Men who brought forth these new interpretations are those we call "Prophets of Modern Hinduism." They range from Ram Mohan Roy (1772–1833) in Bengal to Mahatma Gandhi (1869–1948) in Gujarat. Among the cadres of these prophets, all hailed from the Bengal region, except for two who were from Gujarat: Swami Dayanand (1824–1883) and Gandhi.

Both Dayanand and Gandhi had left far-reaching negative impacts on British Indian politics and politics after the British exodus. While popular thinking that Modern Hinduism is a reformatory movement and therefore a far better alternative to its predecessor is entrenched, we contend it is far more ideologically precarious with its unending mutations. The business of reinterpretation is a never-ending theme among educated Hindus in general and Hindu nationalists in particular. In this role, many educated Hindus manufacture Hinduism (and history) out of thin air suitable to their current situations in the hope that the lie (in the service of Modern Hinduism) will hold sway. This lie can go further. There are those educated Hindus (including its army of missionary monks) who will concoct theories purporting to expand the borders of Hinduism at the expense of other religions and philosophies. Hindu nationalism and its many poisonous tentacles are the children of Modern Hinduism.

Modern Hinduism has seriously undermined the traditional-minded simple Hindus as well as their neighbors, including Christians, Muslims, and Sikhs. This characteristic of Modern Hinduism is essential to unfolding the mystery surrounding the Constitution, especially what transpired immediately after the Constituent Assembly overwhelmingly passed the resolution adopting its final draft copy.

We are thankful to Ravi Shankar Prasad, India's current Minister of Law and Justice, who made it known in a speech delivered in New Delhi on February 17, 2017 that the decision-makers of the Constituent Assembly (possibly not Dr. Ambedkar) decided to incorporate the heritage of India into the final draft document of the Constitution. To achieve this, they sought the services of Nandalal Bose (1882–1966), the famous painter of Bengal. According to the reports gathered, Bose became the principal of the Kala Bhavana (College of Arts) at Tagore's International University Santiniketan in 1922. His credentials are suggestive of a professional man well versed in delivering the artwork consistent with the ideals inspired by Modern Hinduism.

After receiving the final, duly signed copy of the Constitution, Bose took nearly five years to produce the finished product. This beautification process of the Parts of the Constitution, each of which is accompanied by an illustration at its beginning, reflects the past images of India as if approved by those in tally with Modern Hinduism. Prem Behari Narain Raizda did the calligraphy in the book. Once fully beautified, the original copy of the Constitution found a safe resting place in a special helium-filled vault in the Library at the Parliament of India building

Further, Prime Minister Jawaharlal Nehru (1889–1964) hand-picked the same Bose to sketch the emblems for the Government of India's awards, including the *Bharat Ratna* and the *Padma Shri*.

Thanks largely to Minister Prasad, we were able to procure a digital copy of the finished copy of the Constitution, showing the calligraphy as well as the illustrations.

The reader should review Appendix D for the list of illustrations and Appendix E for the twenty-two figures. Look at Figure 15, which shows Guru Gobind Singh (1666–1708) in contrast with Chhatrapati Shivaji (1630–1680) posted on Part XV. Appendix D depicts this illustration as "Muslim Period." What is the significance of adding Guru Gobind Singh to this Constitution? None except that the Hindu nationalists have transformed the Guru into an archetype hero, handsomely portraying him as a savior warrior who once fought against the Muslims to safeguard the beleaguered Hindus during the Mughal era. This is the best example of Modern Hinduism's attempt to subvert history to highlight its ideology. No mention is given that the first people to attack the Guru were Hindu kings themselves and part of the reason they did so was to maintain the caste system.

Another example worthy of examination is Figure 19, where Subhas Chandra Bose (1897–1945) is illuminated at two borders, each with a caption: **"In this Holy War for India's Liberation, We ask for your blessings"** and **"Mahatmaji—Father of our nation."** Are these proclamations made in obeisance to Mahatma Gandhi? Alternatively, do they refer to the sacredness of Subhas Chandra Bose himself? It is not entirely clear. Subhas Chandra Bose, well known as a fascist leader, allied himself during the Second World War first with Adolf Hitler and then with Imperial Japan, set against the Allies in general and British in particular with an objective of defeating them in the subcontinent. In spite of his own defeat, his true history has been subverted in light of Modern Hinduism. It appears that according to this copy of the Constitution, India has two "fathers of the nation" in accordance with the description corresponding to Part XVII in Appendix D and Figure 19 in Appendix

E representing Gandhi and Subhas Chandra Bose, respectively.

Conclusion

My friend says that the last time when I spoke, I said that I wanted to burn the Constitution. Well, in a hurry I did not explain the reason. Now that my friend has given me the opportunity, I think I shall give the reason. The reason is this: We built a temple for a god to come in and reside, but before the god could be installed, if the devil had taken possession of it, what else could we do except destroy the temple? We did not intend that it should be occupied by the Asuras. We intended it to be occupied by the Devas. That is the reason why I said I would rather like to burn it.

—B.R. Ambedkar
March 19, 1955, Rajya Sabha

It is high time to reassess Dr. Ambedkar's role in the making of India's Constitution. While in the Rajya Sabha in 1953, and while addressing and referring to the proceedings of the Constituent Assembly of the past, he made it quite clear that he worked as an agent of those wielding power—no doubt headed by Jawaharlal Nehru. In other words, Ambedkar acted as a front man for the Hindu leaders running the Constituent Assembly debates, and his connection with the making of the Constitution remains only for that short period—roughly three years. Reading the above six chapters of this book should surprise no one that Ambedkar desired to burn this Constitution while announcing that it *"does not suit anybody."*

Regardless of the propaganda generated from different sources, it is obvious that Ambedkar was neither the author nor architect of the Constitution. In his final speech delivered on November 25, 1949, when the final draft of the Constitution came into being, he made this clear when he denied being its drafter. To his great credit, in the beginning days (possibly even before) of the Constituent Assembly, Ambedkar[10] wrote a book titled *States and Minorities: What are their Rights and How to Secure them in the Constitution of Free India* that was published in 1947. Clearly, he aspired to influence the Constituent Assembly debates with a calculated move to protect the rights of those people (Untouchables or the Dalits) he loved most. However, he failed. Right before Ambedkar penned this book, M. N. Roy (1887–1954)—who by the 1940s had matured in his breathtaking revolutionary journey from his extolling Marxism in his early years to promoting "Radical Humanism"—drafted a book titled *Constitution of Free India: A Draft* that was published in 1945. He too sensed that with the upcoming British departure, the colony of British-India would need a new constitution based upon the evolved democratic rights worthy of the ground realities. It appears his genuine attempt, just like that of Ambedkar, to positively influence the Constituent Assembly failed.

In addition to Ambedkar's complete divorce from the Constitution in 1953, something else became clear. While in the Rajya Sabha in 1955, he referred to India's leaders (or its political class) as *"Asuras."* This word comes up profusely in Hindu mythology and simply means *"Demons."* At this juncture, Ambedkar might as well have formally resigned from the Rajya Sabha because his functional links morphed into an atmosphere of humiliations leveled against him from the State and its apparatchiks.

In spirit of their sheer arrogance, these same *Asuras* long after Ambedkar's premature death enacted Forty-Second Amendment Act in 1976 under the heading of "Fundamental Duties":

> **51A.** It shall be the duty of every citizen of India—
>
> (a) to abide by the Constitution and respect its ideals and institutions, the National Flag and the National Anthem;

Any person of India must ask these questions: On what criteria should one abide by the undemocratic provisions of the Constitution? Why would anyone respect its ideals and institutions as reflected in its fake hypocritical ideals, draconian laws, and systemically corrupt institutions?

Furthermore, as is well known, the modern Indian State declared Gandhi its "Father of the Nation." It is evident how much Gandhi influenced the making of the Constitution through his intermediaries running the proceedings of the Constituent Assembly. Gandhi's cherished ideas of:

- deprivation of legal fundamental rights

- establishment of a camouflaged Hindu Totalitarian state

- declaration of Sikhs as Hindus

- declaration of Buddhists as Hindus

- declaration of Jains as Hindus

- surreptitious declaration of Christians and Muslims as Hindus

- consolidation and politicization of the Caste System

- consolidation of the status of Sudras (lowest caste); and

- consolidation of the status of Untouchables (outcastes)[11] were distilled and incorporated into the framework of the Constitution—but not necessarily overtly.

There is another feature that becomes evident when this Constitution is studied carefully through the historical lens of the Government of India Act 1935 and its predecessors. This Act(s) formulated a political framework called "Dyarchy" as an ingenious tool to rule the colonial subjects in British India. Accordingly, there were two levels of the government: the lower level was the Parliament (or State Legislatures) into which the citizens elected their representatives, and the upper level where the unelected Viceroy and his Executive Council presided. The actual power resided with the Viceroy. Structurally speaking, the framework of the Government of India Act of 1935 made its way into the Constitution. In other words, the Dyarchy model described above entered the Constitution. At the lower level, it remains the same as it was before 1947. At the upper level, instead of an unelected Viceroy, there is a Prime Minister who also need not be elected. While the Dyarchy model provides the Constitution with a seemingly strong physical structure, it is at the functional level where truly a change has occurred since the British left. Since then, Modern Hinduism has run the spirit of the Constitution, and this ideology runs the gears of the Constitution-powered government. In addition, its pernicious ideas have filtered to outside spheres of influence including the media, political parties and their subsidiaries, a significant chunk of academia, Bollywood, law enforcement agencies, security-related forces, and many educated sections of the population.

What can the people of India do to reverse this deleterious phase of their Constitution and its history? While we should all ponder over this, it is time to assess what Ambedkar thought of this dilemma. At the Rajya Sabha on March 19, 1955, following his statement as produced at the top conclusion section of the book, B.K.P. Sinha—a fellow member of Rajya Sabha from the State of Bihar—rhetorically replied to Ambedkar, "Destroy the devil rather than the temple." To which, Dr. Ambedkar replied:

> *You can not do it. We have not got the strength. If you*
> *will read the Brahmana, the Sathapatha Brahmana,[12] you*

will see that the gods have always been defeated by the Asuras, and that the Asuras had the Amrit with them which the gods had to take away in order to survive in the battle. Now, Sir, I am being interrupted ...

No doubt Sinha pointed to the Constitution by euphemistically using the word "temple" just as Ambedkar had. It appears Sinha preferred to safeguard the Constitution while concurrently destroying the *Asuras*. It also appears that Ambedkar did not agree with him. Why?

As an antidote to the Constitution and India's political elite, Ambedkar would have us believe what? Nothing! Are the people of India doomed forever in the bosom of Hinduism? Is the Constitution a bogeyman for Hinduism in action or just its front persona in camouflage? If *Asuras* (the political class) run the political show of Hinduism, then what avenues are open for anyone to safeguard himself or herself from the hovering and impending dangers? Apparently, none, in the eyes of Ambedkar.[13] Think about it. While the people of India are literally stranded in the unhealthy political landscape with no escape, those holding powers and espousing vested interests celebrate without any sense of shame the legacy of Dr. Ambedkar with pomp and show via ritually linking his prestigious public standing with the Constitution of India!

In light of what has been presented in the above chapters, we must ask this question: Does the Indian Constitution espouse democratic, authoritarian, or totalitarian values? Without a shadow of doubt, we can conclude India is not a democratic country. The sooner we realize this fact, the easier will it be to handle the difficult issues faced by the poverty-stricken masses of India in the future. How deeply ingrained India is within the ideological frameworks of authoritarianism (or even totalitarianism) is left up to the readers and political scholars to evaluate, along with its associated links with Modern Hinduism.

Appendix A

PART III

FUNDAMENTAL RIGHTS

General

12. In this Part, unless the context otherwise requires, "the State" includes the Government and Parliament of India and the Government and the Legislature of each of the States and all local or other authorities within the territory of India or under the control of the Government of India.

13. **(1)** All laws in force in the territory of India immediately before the commencement of this Constitution, in so far as they are inconsistent with the provisions of this Part, shall, to the extent of such inconsistency, be void.

(2) The State shall not make any law which takes away or abridges the rights conferred by this Part and any law made in contravention of this clause shall, to the extent of the contravention, be void.

(3) In this article, unless the context otherwise requires,—

(a) "law" includes any Ordinance, order, bye-law, rule, regulation, notification, custom or usage having in the territory of India the force of law;

(b) "laws in force" includes laws passed or made by a Legislature or other competent authority in the territory of India before the commencement of this Constitution and not previously repealed, notwithstanding that any such law or any part thereof may not be then in operation either at all or in particular areas.

(4) Nothing in this article shall apply to any amendment of this Constitution made under article 368.

Right to Equality

14. The State shall not deny to any person equality before the law or the equal protection of the laws within the territory of India.

15. (1) The State shall not discriminate against any citizen on grounds only of religion, race, caste, sex, place of birth or any of them.

(2) No citizen shall, on grounds only of religion, race, caste, sex, place of birth or any of them, be subject to any disability, liability, restriction or condition with regard to—

(a) access to shops, public restaurants, hotels and places of public entertainment; or

(b) the use of wells, tanks, bathing ghats, roads and places of public resort maintained wholly or partly out of State funds or dedicated to the use of the general public.

(3) Nothing in this article shall prevent the State from making any special provision for women and children.

(4) Nothing in this article or in clause (2) of article 29 shall prevent the State from making any special provision for the advancement of any socially and educationally backward classes of citizens or for the Scheduled Castes and the Scheduled Tribes.

(5) Nothing in this article or in sub-clause (g) of clause (1) of article 19 shall prevent the State from making any special provision, by law, for the advancement of any socially and educationally backward classes of citizens or for the Scheduled Castes or the Scheduled Tribes in so far as such special provisions relate to their admission to educational institutions including private educational institutions, whether aided or unaided by the State, other than the minority educational institutions referred to in clause

(1) of article 30.

16. **(1)** There shall be equality of opportunity for all citizens in matters relating to employment or appointment to any office under the State.

(2) No citizen shall, on grounds only of religion, race, caste, sex, descent, place of birth, residence or any of them, be ineligible for, or discriminated against in respect of, any employment or office under the State.

(3) Nothing in this article shall prevent Parliament from making any law prescribing, in regard to a class or classes of employment or appointment to an office under the Government of, or any local or other authority within, a State or Union territory, any requirement as to residence within that State or Union territory prior to such employment or appointment.

(4) Nothing in this article shall prevent the State from making any provision for the reservation of appointments or posts in favour of any backward class of citizens which, in the opinion of the State, is not adequately represented in the services under the State.

(4A) Nothing in this article shall prevent the State from making any provision for reservation in matters of promotion, with consequential seniority, to any class or classes of posts in the services under the State in favour of the Scheduled Castes and the Scheduled Tribes which, in the opinion of the State, are not adequately represented in the services under the State.

(4B) Nothing in this article shall prevent the State from considering any unfilled vacancies of a year which are reserved for being filled up in that year in accordance with any provision for reservation made under clause (4) or clause (4A) as a separate class of vacancies to be filled up in any succeeding year or years and such class of vacancies shall not be considered together with the vacancies of the year in which they are being filled up for determining the ceiling of fifty per cent. reservation on total number of vacancies of that year.

(5) Nothing in this article shall affect the operation of any law which provides that the incumbent of an office in connection with the affairs of any religious or denominational institution or any member of the governing body thereof shall be a person professing a particular religion or belonging to a particular denomination.

17. "Untouchability" is abolished and its practice in any form is forbidden. The enforcement of any disability arising out of "Untouchability" shall be an offence punishable in accordance with law.

18. (1) No title, not being a military or academic distinction, shall be conferred by the State.

(2) No citizen of India shall accept any title from any foreign State.

(3) No person who is not a citizen of India shall, while he holds any office of profit or trust under the State, accept without the consent of the President any title from any foreign State.

(4) No person holding any office of profit or trust under the State shall, without the consent of the President, accept any present, emolument, or office of any kind from or under any foreign State.

Right to Freedom

19. (1) All citizens shall have the right——

(a) to freedom of speech and expression;

(b) to assemble peaceably and without arms;

(c) to form associations or unions;

(d) to move freely throughout the territory of India;

(e) to reside and settle in any part of the territory of India; and

(g) to practise any profession, or to carry on any occupation, trade or business.

(2) Nothing in sub-clause (a) of clause (1) shall affect the operation of any existing law, or prevent the State from making any law, in so far as such law imposes reasonable restrictions on the exercise of the right conferred by the said sub-clause in the interests of the sovereignty and integrity of India, the security of the State, friendly relations with foreign States, public order, decency or morality, or in relation to contempt of court, defamation or incitement to an offence.

(3) Nothing in sub-clause (b) of the said clause shall affect the operation of any existing law in so far as it imposes, or prevent the State from making any law imposing, in the interests of the sovereignty and integrity of India or public order, reasonable restrictions on the exercise of the right conferred by the said sub-clause.

(4) Nothing in sub-clause (c) of the said clause shall affect the operation of any existing law in so far as it imposes, or prevent the State from making any law imposing, in the interests of the sovereignty and integrity of India or public order or morality, reasonable restrictions on the exercise of the right conferred by the said sub-clause.

(5) Nothing in sub-clauses (d) and (e) of the said clause shall affect the operation of any existing law in so far as it imposes, or prevent the State from making any law imposing, reasonable restrictions on the exercise of any of the rights conferred by the said sub-clauses either in the interests of the general public or for the protection of the interests of any Scheduled Tribe.

(6) Nothing in sub-clause (g) of the said clause shall affect the operation of any existing law in so far as it imposes, or prevent the State from making any law imposing, in the interests of the general public, reasonable restrictions on the exercise of the right conferred by the said sub-clause, and, in particular, nothing in the said sub-clause shall affect the operation of any existing law in so far as it relates to, or prevent the State from making any law relating to,——

(i) the professional or technical qualifications necessary for practising any profession or carrying on any occupation, trade or business, or

(ii) the carrying on by the State, or by a corporation owned or controlled by the State, of any trade, business, industry or service, whether to the exclusion, complete or partial, of citizens or otherwise.

20. **(1)** No person shall be convicted of any offence except for violation of a law in force at the time of the commission of the Act charged as an offence, nor be subjected to a penalty greater than that which might have been inflicted under the law in force at the time of the commission of the offence.

(2) No person shall be prosecuted and punished for the same offence more than once.

(3) No person accused of any offence shall be compelled to be a witness against himself.

21. No person shall be deprived of his life or personal liberty except according to procedure established by law.

21A. The State shall provide free and compulsory education to all children of the age of six to fourteen years in such manner as the State may, by law, determine.

22. **(1)** No person who is arrested shall be detained in custody without being informed, as soon as may be, of the grounds for such arrest nor shall he be denied the right to consult, and to be defended by, a legal practitioner of his choice.

(2) Every person who is arrested and detained in custody shall be produced before the nearest magistrate within a period of twenty-four hours of such arrest excluding the time necessary for the journey from the place of arrest to the court of the magistrate and no such person shall be detained in custody beyond the said period without the authority of a magistrate.

(3) Nothing in clauses (1) and (2) shall apply—

(a) to any person who for the time being is an enemy alien; or

(b) to any person who is arrested or detained under any law providing for preventive detention.

(4) No law providing for preventive detention shall authorise the detention of a person for a longer period than three months unless—

(a) an Advisory Board consisting of persons who are, or have been, or are qualified to be appointed as, Judges of a High Court has reported before the expiration of the said period of three months that there is in its opinion sufficient cause for such detention:

Provided that nothing in this sub-clause shall authorise the detention of any person beyond the maximum period prescribed by any law made by Parliament under sub-clause (b) of clause (7); or

(b) such person is detained in accordance with the provisions of any law made by Parliament under sub-clauses (a) and (b) of clause (7).

(5) When any person is detained in pursuance of an order made under any law providing for preventive detention, the authority making the order shall, as soon as may be, communicate to such person the grounds on which the order has been made and shall afford him the earliest opportunity of making a representation against the order.

(6) Nothing in clause (5) shall require the authority making any such order as is referred to in that clause to disclose facts which such authority considers to be against the public interest to disclose.

(7) Parliament may by law prescribe—

(a) the circumstances under which, and the class or classes of cases in which, a person may be detained for a period longer than three months under any law providing for preventive detention without obtaining the opinion of an Advisory Board in accordance with the provisions of sub-clause (a) of clause (4);

(b) the maximum period for which any person may in any class or classes of cases be detained under any law providing for preventive detention; and

(c) the procedure to be followed by an Advisory Board in an inquiry under sub-clause (a) of clause (4).

Right against Exploitation

23. **(1)** Traffic in human beings and *begar* and other similar forms of forced labour are prohibited and any contravention of this provision shall be an offence punishable in accordance with law.

(2) Nothing in this article shall prevent the State from imposing compulsory service for public purposes, and in imposing such service the State shall not make any discrimination on grounds only of religion, race, caste or class or any of them.

Right to Freedom of Religion

25. **(1)** Subject to public order, morality and health and to the other provisions of this Part, all persons are equally entitled to freedom of conscience and the right freely to profess, practise and propagate religion.

(2) Nothing in this article shall affect the operation of any existing law or prevent the State from making any law—

(a) regulating or restricting any economic, financial, political or other secular activity which may be associated with religious practice;

(b) providing for social welfare and reform or the throwing open of Hindu religious institutions of a public character to all classes and sections of Hindus.

Explanation I.—The wearing and carrying of *kirpans* shall be deemed to be included in the profession of the Sikh religion.

Explanation II.—In sub-clause (b) of clause (2), the refer-ence to Hindus shall be construed as including a reference to persons professing the Sikh, Jaina or Buddhist religion, and the reference to Hindu religious institutions shall be construed accordingly.

26. Subject to public order, morality and health, every religious denomination or any section thereof shall have the right—

(a) to establish and maintain institutions for religious and charitable purposes;

(b) to manage its own affairs in matters of religion;

(c) to own and acquire movable and immovable prop-erty; and

(d) to administer such property in accordance with law.

27. No person shall be compelled to pay any taxes, the proceeds of which are specifically appropriated in pay-ment of expenses for the promotion or maintenance of any particular religion or religious denomination.

28. **(1)** No religious instruction shall be provided in any educational institution wholly maintained out of State funds.

(2) Nothing in clause (1) shall apply to an educational institution which is administered by the State but has been established under any endowment or trust which requires that religious instruction shall be imparted in such institu-tion.

(3) No person attending any educational institution recognised by the State or receiving aid out of State funds shall be required to take part in any religious instruction that may be imparted in such institution or to attend any religious worship that may be conducted in such institution or in any premises attached thereto unless such person or, if such person is a minor, his guardian has given his consent thereto.

Cultural and Educational Rights

29. **(1)** Any section of the citizens residing in the territory of India or any part thereof having a distinct language, script or culture of its own shall have the right to conserve the same.

(2) No citizen shall be denied admission into any educational institution maintained by the State or receiving aid out of State funds on grounds only of religion, race, caste, language or any of them.

30. **(1)** All minorities, whether based on religion or language, shall have the right to establish and administer educational institutions of their choice.

(1A) In making any law providing for the compulsory acquisition of any property of an educational institution established and administered by a minority, referred to in clause (1), the State shall ensure that the amount fixed by or determined under such law for the acquisition of such property is such as would not restrict or abrogate the right guaranteed under that clause.

(2) The State shall not, in granting aid to educational institutions, discriminate against any educational institution on the ground that it is under the management of a minority, whether based on religion or language.

31. [*Compulsory acquisition of property.*] *Rep. by the Constitution (Forty-fourth Amendment) Act, 1978, s. 6 (w.e.f. 20-6-1979).*

31A. **(1)** Notwithstanding anything contained in article 13, no law providing for—

(a) the acquisition by the State of any estate or of any rights therein or the extinguishment or modification of any such rights, or

(b) the taking over of the management of any property by the State for a limited period either in the public interest or in order to secure the proper management of the property, or

(c) the amalgamation of two or more corporations either in the public interest or in order to secure the proper management of any of the corporations, or

(d) the extinguishment or modification of any rights of managing agents, secretaries and treasurers, managing directors, directors or managers of corporations, or of any voting rights of shareholders thereof, or

(e) the extinguishment or modification of any rights accruing by virtue of any agreement, lease or licence for the purpose of searching for, or winning, any mineral or mineral oil, or the premature termination or cancellation of any such agreement, lease or licence,

shall be deemed to be void on the ground that it is inconsistent with, or takes away or abridges any of the rights conferred by article 14 or article 19:

Provided that where such law is a law made by the Legislature of a State, the provisions of this article shall not apply thereto unless such law, having been reserved for the consideration of the President, has received his assent:

Provided further that where any law makes any provision for the acquisition by the State of any estate and where any land comprised therein is held by a person under his personal cultivation, it shall not be lawful for the State to acquire any portion of such land as is within the ceiling limit applicable to him under any law for the time being in force or any building or structure standing thereon or appurtenant thereto, unless the law relating to the acquisition of such land, building or structure, provides for payment of compensation at a rate which shall not be less than the market value thereof.

(2) In this article,—

(a) the expression "estate" shall, in relation to any local area, have the same meaning as that expression or its local equivalent has in the existing law relating to land tenures in force in that area and shall also include—

(i) any *jagir, inam* or *muafi* or other similar grant and in the States of Tamil Nadu and Kerala, any *janmam* right;

(ii) any land held under ryotwari settlement;

(iii) any land held or let for purposes of agriculture or for purposes ancillary thereto, including waste land, forest land, land for pasture or sites of buildings and other structures occupied by cultivators of land, agricultural labourers and village artisans;

(b) the expression "rights", in relation to an estate, shall include any rights vesting in a proprietor, sub-proprietor, under-proprietor, tenure-holder, *raiyat, under-raiyat* or other intermediary and any rights or privileges in respect of land revenue.

31B. Without prejudice to the generality of the provisions contained in article 31A, none of the Acts and Regulations specified in the Ninth Schedule nor any of the provisions thereof shall be deemed to be void, or ever to have become void, on the ground that such Act, Regulation or provision is inconsistent with, or takes away or abridges any of the rights conferred by, any provisions of this Part, and notwithstanding any judgment, decree or order of any court or Tribunal to the contrary, each of the said Acts and Regulations shall, subject to the power of any competent Legislature to repeal or amend it, continue in force.

31C. Notwithstanding anything contained in article 13, no law giving effect to the policy of the State towards securing all or any of the principles laid down in Part IV shall be deemed to be void on the ground that it is inconsistent with, or takes away or abridges any of the rights conferred by article 14 or article 19; *and no law containing a declaration that it is for giving effect to such policy shall be called in question in any court on the ground that it does not give effect to such policy*

Provided that where such law is made by the Legislature of a State, the provisions of this article shall not apply thereto unless such law, having been reserved for the consideration of the President, has received his assent.

31D. [*Saving of laws in respect of anti-national activities.*] *Rep. by the Constitution (Forty-third Amendment) Act, 1977, s. 2 (w.e.f. 13-4-1978).*

Right to Constitutional Remedies

32. (1) The right to move the Supreme Court by appropriate proceedings for the enforcement of the rights conferred by this Part is guaranteed.

(2) The Supreme Court shall have power to issue directions or orders or writs, including writs in the nature of *habeas corpus, mandamus, prohibition, quo warranto* and *certiorari*, whichever may be appropriate, for the enforcement of any of the rights conferred by this Part.

(3) Without prejudice to the powers conferred on the Supreme Court by clauses (1) and (2), Parliament may by law empower any other court to exercise within the local limits of its jurisdiction all or any of the powers exercisable by the Supreme Court under clause (2).

(4) The right guaranteed by this article shall not be suspended except as otherwise provided for by this Constitution.

32A. [*Constitutional validity of State laws not to be considered in proceedings under article 32.*] *Rep. by the Constitution (Forty-third Amendment) Act, 1977, s. 3 (w.e.f. 13-4-1978*

33. Parliament may, by law, determine to what extent any of the rights conferred by this Part shall, in their application to,—

(a) the members of the Armed Forces; or

(b) the members of the Forces charged with the maintenance of public order; or

(c) persons employed in any bureau or other organisa-

tion established by the State for purposes of intelligence or counter intelligence; or

(d) person employed in, or in connection with, the telecommunication systems set up for the purposes of any Force, bureau or organisation referred to in clauses (a) to (c),

be restricted or abrogated so as to ensure the proper discharge of their duties and the maintenance of discipline among them.

34. Notwithstanding anything in the foregoing provisions of this Part, Parliament may by law indemnify any person in the service of the Union or of a State or any other person in respect of any act done by him in connection with the maintenance or restoration of order in any area within the territory of India where martial law was in force or validate any sentence passed, punishment inflicted, forfeiture ordered or other act done under martial law in such area

35. Notwithstanding anything in this Constitution,—

(a) Parliament shall have, and the Legislature of a State shall not have, power to make laws—

(i) with respect to any of the matters which under clause (3) of article 16, clause (3) of article 32, article 33 and article 34 may be provided for by law made by Parliament; and

(ii) for prescribing punishment for those acts which are declared to be offences under this Part; and Parliament shall, as soon as may be after the commencement of this Constitution, make laws for prescribing punishment for the acts referred to in sub-clause (ii);

(b) any law in force immediately before the commencement of this Constitution in the territory of India with respect to any of the matters referred to in sub-clause (i) of clause (a) or providing for punishment for any act referred to in sub-clause (ii) of that clause shall, subject to the terms thereof and to any adaptations and modifications that may be made therein under article 372, continue in force until altered or repealed or amended by Parliament.

Explanation.—In this article, the expression "law in force" has the same meaning as in article 372.

Appendix B

"Bill of Rights" in the Constitution of India[14]
By: G.B. Singh

Introduction

Many admirers of India often go out of their way to depict the country as the "world's largest democracy" and a "secular" state, which through its Constitution guarantees fundamental human rights to all Indians—the implication being that such rights are in practice as a matter of course. Yet dismaying as it may seem, I have never come across any piece of written information analyzing the Constitution, let alone all those enshrined fundamental rights that it guarantees to its citizens. Coupled with aggressive Soviet-style "active measures" channeled by the Indian government, several intellectuals outside India have fallen prey to the media hype. Included on this list are the key members of U.S. Department of State who, upon my inquiry a few years ago, had not even seen what the Constitution looked like, let alone read it! Our academia-based "India Watchers" and think-tank specialists have also dismally failed to undertake the task of assessing the contents of the Indian constitution independently. Instead, what I have noticed is this: they just parrot what they pick from other sources without checking the facts.

Before analyzing the rights enshrined in the Constitution, a few words about it would be helpful to readers. The Constitution (promulgated in 1950) is the longest ever written. As of December 2007, it comprised 395 articles, 12 schedules, 2 Appendices, and

94 amendments. Included on this list are amendments of previous amendments—each amendment often encompasses multiple smaller amendments within its charter. India's Constitution can safely be characterized as one of the most complicated of all modern political documents.

Highly placed Indians with some insight into their Constitution will often take delight in saying that it is based on sound fundamental principles derived from the constitutions of no less than five great Western democracies: Australia, Canada, England, Ireland, and of course, the United States. It all sounds great. Even more impressive is the claim that the Bill of Rights of the U.S. Constitution has made its way into the Indian Constitution. This is always followed by a note of special thanks to the framers of India's Constitution, with singular tribute paid to the likes of Dr. Ambedkar, who chaired the Drafting Committee that created it. But are all these things true?

To answer that question, one must at least procure the most recent copy of the Indian Constitution, read it, understand it, and present the facts as they stand. I did exactly that, which is why I am writing this article.

I hope the reader is familiar with the first ten amendments (known as the Bill of Rights) of the U.S. Constitution, which were ratified in 1791. This information is important because these rights were purportedly imported into the Indian Constitution. For the purpose of this article, it is helpful to reproduce the First Amendment to the U.S. Constitution, which states:

> Congress shall make no law respecting an establishment of religion, or prohibiting the free exercise thereof; or abridging the freedom of speech, or of the press, or the right of the people peaceably to assemble, and to petition the Government for a redress of grievances.

The Substance

Part III of the Indian Constitution (articles 12 through 35) constitutes the entire list of fundamental rights. Of these, total of twenty-four articles, Articles 19 and 25 are the only ones that truly correspond to the First Amendment of the U.S. Constitution. Allow me to reproduce Article 19 in its entirety:

19. **(1)** All citizens shall have the right—

(a) to freedom of speech and expression;

(b) to assemble peaceably and without arms;

(c) to form associations or unions;

(d) to move freely throughout the territory of India;

(e) to reside and settle in any part of the territory of India; and

(g) to practise any profession, or to carry on any occupation, trade or business.

(2) Nothing in sub-clause (a) of clause (1) shall affect the operation of any existing law, or prevent the State from making any law, in so far as such law imposes reasonable restrictions on the exercise of the right conferred by the said sub-clause in the interests of the sovereignty and integrity of India, the security of the State, friendly relations with foreign States, public order, decency or morality, or in relation to contempt of court, defamation or incitement to an offence.

(3) Nothing in sub-clause (b) of the said clause shall affect the operation of any existing law in so far as it imposes, or prevent the State from making any law imposing, in the interests of the sovereignty and integrity of India or public order, reasonable restrictions on the exercise of the right conferred by the said sub-clause.

(4) Nothing in sub-clause (c) of the said clause shall affect the operation of any existing law in so far as it imposes, or prevent the State from making any law imposing, in the interests of the sovereignty and integrity of India or public order or morality, reasonable restrictions on the exercise of the right conferred by the said sub-clause.

(5) Nothing in sub-clauses (d) and (e) of the said clause shall affect the operation of any existing law in so far as

it imposes, or prevent the State from making any law imposing, reasonable restrictions on the exercise of any of the
rights conferred by the said sub-clauses either in the interests of the general public or for the protection of the interests of any Scheduled Tribe.

(6) Nothing in sub-clause (g) of the said clause shall affect the operation of any existing law in so far as it imposes,
or prevent the State from making any law imposing, in the
interests of the general public, reasonable restrictions on
the exercise of the right conferred by the said sub-clause,
and, in particular, nothing in the said sub-clause shall affect the operation of any existing law in so far as it relates to, or prevent the State from making any law relating
to,——

(i) the professional or technical qualifications necessary for practising any profession or carrying on any occupation, trade or business, or

(ii) the carrying on by the State, or by a corporation
owned or controlled by the State, of any trade, business,
industry or service, whether to the exclusion, complete
or partial, of citizens or otherwise.

Although much of the above narrative is redundant, nobody
doubts the clarity of Clause 1 of Article 19. However, everything
changes with what is written in Clause 2 and onward. For all practical purposes, the fundamental rights given in Clause 1 have been
nibbled away one by one, thanks to Clauses 2 through 6. The reader
must have noticed that Clause 1(f), which had been "to acquire, hold
and dispose of property" is missing. The Forty-fourth Amendment
expunged that portion in 1978, most likely enacted to bring political
India in accordance with Communism at a time when the Soviet
Union was its close ally. Things get even more complicated in articles 352 through 360 of the Indian Constitution, which essentially
deliver the Emergency Provisions. Because numerous geographical
areas of India frequently have fallen under these provisions to
yield to the President's rule, the reality of the fundamental rights
supposedly guaranteed under Article 19 and others shows that

citizens have been forced to live under draconian laws.

What makes the problem even more tendentious is that according to the Fortieth Amendment, such draconian laws may not be challenged before any court on the grounds that they violate fundamental rights. If one or more groups of people have suffered terribly from the repressive hands of the State, the Forty-first Amendment stifles any potential litigant. It provides that the President, Prime Minister, and State Governors are immune from criminal prosecution for life and from civil prosecution during their term of office. What about the press in India? It exercises its freedom of speech, as the apologists reminds us with regularity. Nevertheless, the facts are otherwise. Indian journalists have learned too well how to kowtow to the ruling Indian leaders.

Now, let us look at Article 25:

25. **(1)** Subject to public order, morality and health and to the other provisions of this Part, all persons are equally entitled to freedom of conscience and the right freely to profess, practise and propagate religion.

(2) Nothing in this article shall affect the operation of any existing law or prevent the State from making any law—

(a) regulating or restricting any economic, financial, political or other secular activity which may be associated with religious practice;

(b) providing for social welfare and reform or the throwing open of Hindu religious institutions of a public character to all classes and sections of Hindus.

Explanation I.—The wearing and carrying of *kirpans* shall be deemed to be included in the profession of the Sikh religion.

Explanation II.—In sub-clause (b) of clause (2), the reference to Hindus shall be construed as including a reference to persons professing the Sikh, Jaina or Buddhist religion, and the reference to Hindu religious institutions shall be construed accordingly.

In a historical sense, Article 25 is unique. Even though Hindu hands wrote it following the British departure in 1947, future Hindu hands have spared it thus far from additional amendment. Those responsible for writing Article 25 were no less cunning and deceptive—they knew how to shelter it behind the barrage of words only a few could understand. I have attempted to unravel the mystery of Article 25 to the best of my abilities.

Teachings such as peaceful coexistence, high morals, high ethical values, and respect for fellow humans are integral to any true religion. Given that, why is religious freedom in India contingent upon factors of public order, morality, and health in Clause 1? Is there such a religion that violates the norms of decent human morality? If indeed there is any such religion, one would think the framers of the Indian Constitution would have alerted us or perhaps would have banned it. Would Hinduism, Islam, or for that matter any other religion falls under that category?

With Hindu leaders in charge of Hindu India, the name of the game is unchecked fundamentalist Hinduism, however undesirable it might be to a reasonable mind. But during British India, this fundamentalism came very close to being curbed, as recorded in a superbly written book—*Mother India* by Katherine Mayo (Greenwood Press Publishers, 1927)—which states:

> *It is true that, to conform to the International Convention for the Suppression of the Circulation of and Traffic in Obscene Publications, signed in Geneva on September 12, 1923, the Indian Legislature duly amended the Indian Penal Code and Code of Criminal Procedure; and that this amendment duly prescribes set penalties for "whoever sells, lets to hire, distributes, publicly exhibits ... conveys ... or receives profit from any obscene object, book, representation or figure." But its enactment unqualified, although welcome to the Muhammadans, would have wrought havoc with the religious belongings, the ancient traditions and customs and the priestly prerogatives dear to the Hindu majority. Therefore the Indian Legislature, preponderantly Hindu, saddled the*

amendment with an exception, which reads:

This section does not extend to any book, pamphlet, writing, drawing or painting kept or used bona fide for religious purposes or any represented sculptured, engraved, painted or otherwise represented on or in any temple, or on any car used for the conveyance of idols, or kept or used for any religious purpose.

To conclude, in India, the freedom to practice religion is conditional at best. The power to interpret and exercise the conditional requirements is in the hands of Hindu leaders and nobody else. This is radically different from the United States, where the practice of religion is a free, unconditional right. Conversely, in modern India, the practice of religion is a politician-sanctioned, unreliable right.

Clause 2(a) of Article 25 is muddy at best. Considering the constitutional phrasing, it seems religion is composed of economic, political, and worship activities. Anything other than worship activity is termed "secular." Therefore, in accordance with the Constitution, the Indian State has the right to interfere with those activities of the church it considers "secular." The church—structure included—is an economic venture after all. In a socialist country such as India, organized religions (Christianity, Islam, Sikhism, etc.) with large groups of people interacting among themselves and others amounts to nothing less than political activity. Any propagation of religion will require several "secular" tasks: financial, organizational, and personnel activities (just to name a few).

The Indian State can constitutionally restrict any one or all of these "secular" endeavors, thereby effectively hampering the genuine propagation of any religion it desires. This has already happened, as illustrated in another fine book: *Soft State: A Newspaperman's Chronicle of India* by Bernard D. Nossiter (Harper & Row Publishers, 1970). I suppose one way to safeguard from State incursion is to worship in the open air (which will ensure no economic activity) or alone within the confines of a house (which will ensure no political activity). How anyone worships individually in these conditions may be beyond the Indian State's intrusive nature! That's my hope!

Now, consider Clause 2(b). What does freedom of religion have to do with social welfare and reform? This sub-clause contains a statement with strange wording that needs scrutiny. First, are Hindu religious institutions of a public character? This term is ambiguous and could mean literally anything or absolutely nothing. My gut feeling is that it pertains to Hindu schools, the temples, and ashrams. Second, what does the reference to "classes" of Hindus mean? This is an inappropriate Western term about the Hindu society. Nonetheless, if the term must be used, the majority of the Hindu population falls into the low class while the minority belongs to the middle and upper classes. Third, what are the "sections" of Hindus? At the lowest common denominator, the bulk of Hindu sections comprise the Vaishnava, Saiva, and Sakti.

The State can regulate the opening of Hindu temples, schools, and/or ashrams to all high, middle, or low Hindu classes irrespective of whether one is Vaishnava, Saiva, Sakti, or what have you. This interpretation may be off the mark if I am reading incorrectly because of the use of terms that are vague. Unfortunately, the framers of the Constitution missed the crux of the problem.

The Hindu society is governed by caste (or *varna*) and not just necessarily by the classes and sections. A caste is not the same thing as a class or section. If you feel that the framers of the Constitution were themselves not sure of what they wrote or its underlying meaning, they perhaps hoped that the reader would be reassured in the offering of *Explanation I* and *Explanation II*. At this juncture, I am reminded the abrupt change in the narrative of Article 25. Hardly a surprise here, however, but it triggers any thinking person well read in Hinduism to chart the similarities one encounters after carefully reading Hindu scriptures. For example, in the *Bhagavad Gita*, it is not uncommon to see a transition from one topic to another that is disconcertingly abrupt. I am afraid this is clearly the case in Article 25.

Explanation I and *Explanation II* are not even remotely connected with Clause 2(b). The fact is that they urgently call for explanations of their own. *Explanation I* acknowledge the existence of the Sikh religion. However, since the issue is the individual religious rights (in Sikhism), the proper word ought to be *"kirpan,"* not *"kirpans."* Moreover, *Explanation II* is notoriously flawed. Its intent is obvious: the individual members of Sikh, Jain, and Buddhist religions will be referred to as Hindus, and thus Sikhism, Jainism, and Buddhism are retroactively to be considered inseparable sects of Hinduism. Therefore, the State can interfere with their religious institutions as it sees fit under the guise of procuring "social reforms."

Because the Constitution refuses to delve further, one might ask: Is there a definition or an explanation of what constitute Hinduism? And who really is a Hindu? Answering these questions has been anything but easy in part because both these terms—"Hindu" and "Hinduism"—are entirely absent from their varied scriptures and were promulgated by their colonial masters, both Islamic and British. Scholars over the years have tried their best but failed to address these terms adequately. Of late, the Supreme Court has pitched in. For example, the Court observed in 1965 that the term "Hindu" referred to "the orthodox Hindu religion which recognizes castes and contains injunctions [based] on caste distinctions." By 1966, the Court stepped in further. Rather than defining the issue, it issued broad guidelines—three different "standpoints" which require an art and gift application—which can be conveniently adapted to the circumstances. They are worth reading:

First Standpoint:

> *We find it difficult, if not impossible, to define Hindu religion or even adequately describe it. Unlike other religions in the world, the Hindu religion does not claim any one prophet; it does not worship any one God; it does not subscribe to any one dogma; it does not believe in any one philosophic concept; it does not follow any one set of religious rites or performances; in fact, it does not appear to satisfy the narrow traditional [for traditional, read Western] features of any religion or creed. It may broadly be described as a way of life and nothing more.*[15]

This is confusing because it fails to ascertain whether one is a Hindu. To clarify further, the Court introduced the second guideline.

Second Standpoint:

> *Beneath the diversity of Hindu philosophy, the Court found, "lie certain broad concepts which are treated as basic."*

Those broad concepts are: (a) Acceptance of the Vedas as the highest authority in religious and philosophic matters; (b) The great world rhythms; and (c) Rebirth and pre-existence. Having pinpointed the "unity" of the creed here, then the Court proceeded to address the final guideline.

Third Standpoint:

> *Addressing the often asked insidious philosophic question as to what is the "ultimate goal of humanity", the Court answered, "It is release and freedom from the unceasing cycle of births and rebirths ... "*

Religious literature would call this goal "salvation." However, salvation is something pointing to an individual person and not necessarily addressing the collective sense of humanity. Perhaps after recognizing that the Court potentially might open a can of worms, it left the burgeoning issue unanswered by agreeing "there is a great divergence of views."

Rather than adequately resolving the given problem of the meaning of the terms "Hindu" and "Hinduism," the Court's interjection complicated the matter, and it therefore needed a quick rescue. In searching for the "working formula," they found in the person of B.G. Tilak (1856–1920), a fiery, politically drenched, fundamentalist Hindu, who apparently had once prescribed: *"the acceptance of the Vedas with reverence, recognition, of the fact that the means or ways of salvation are diverse; realization of the truth that the number of gods to be worshipped is large."*[16] In the end, thanks to the Court, "Hindu" and "Hinduism" are false terms bounded by the foundational hierarchy-arranged caste and aided by the doctrines of karma and reincarnation as its supporting outer boundaries. Inside this rather large hierarchical triangular entity, the framework is supported by myriad pillars that tighten and cement the construction. These include worshipping an army of gods and goddesses, incredible loads of superstitions and rituals, yoga, Ayurveda, corruption, immoralities, inflicting human-rights abuses, self-inflicted psychology guaranteeing brainwashing, a totalitarian mode of life, realpolitik and war. The list is long. It's not too difficult to imagine that separating oneself from Hindu conditioning is next to impossible. If you think you have been let down by India's Supreme Court in resolving this matter, then you may receive a further shock: Hindu politicians and their followers continue to be willfully negligent in their refusals to add any needed clarity. Incredibly, in recent years, a Senior Advocate named, Samaraditya Pal, in his multiple volumes addressing the Indian Constitution article-by-article, summed up the mystery of Hinduism as per above cited Court case:

- It is difficult to define Hindu religion or even adequately describe it.

- Hinduism does not appear to satisfy the narrow traditional features of any religion.

- It may broadly be described as a way of life and nothing more.

- It is based on the idea of universal receptivity.

- Persons belonging to Swaminarayan Sampradaya (Sects) are also Hindus.[17]

Also recently there has surfaced further insight into Hinduism, in 2011—this time, the Punjab and Haryana High Court pronounced its verdict on a case filed by two Sikh petitioners against the misuse of the word "Hindu" applying on the very personal identity of Sikh people portrayed within the charter of four named Hindu Code Bills, later enacted as laws: (1) Hindu Succession Act, 1956; (2) Hindu Marriage Act, 1955; (3) Hindu Adoption and Maintenance Act, 1956; and (4) Hindu Minority and Guardianship Act. 1956. While denying the petitioners their case, the Court defined Hinduism as: "Hinduism, as we have been made to understand by scholars and sages at different times and different ages is not a strait jacket religion; it is a way of life. It is a 'Dharma'. Hindus are not one people but many. Therein lies the beauty of India." One can see how insufficient and pathetic this definition of Hinduism is apart from being irrational and illogical.

Like the Sikhs, the Jain community too has been vocal in its denunciation of Article 25. Recently, it has come to my attention that they sought an understanding from then-Prime Minister Jawaharlal Nehru. In response, Nehru's Principal Private Secretary, A.V. Pai, (writing for his boss) penned the followings words for the benefit of Jains, dated January 31, 1950:

> *This Article [25] merely makes a definition. This definition by enforcing a specific constitutional arrangement circumscribes that rule. Likewise, you will note that this mentions not only Jains but also Buddhists and Sikhs. It is clear that Buddhists are not Hindus and therefore there need to be no apprehension that the Jains are designated as Hindus. There is no doubt that the Jains are a different religious community and this accepted position is in no way affected by the constitution.*

Again, it is hardly a surprise to see how illogical and evasive the above clarification is! Why do the educated Hindus placed high in political positions speak from both sides of their mouths? Why can't they simply amend the controversial Article 25 to reflect the religious rights truly? Why would they continue to exercise deceptive means to declare non-Hindus to be Hindus and yet never define what Hinduism means in the first place?

In August 2005, continuing to address the ongoing issue of personal religious identities affecting the Jains, the Supreme Court refused to grant any relief to religious minority communities (in this case both Sikhs and Jains) from being bracketed under the label of Hindu.

The word "secularism" is often invoked diligently by the caste Hindus when describing the Indian State in the spirit of nationalistic Hinduism, with an underlying implication of the Hindu expansionist quest to absorb other religions. The Western definition of "secularism" is when the State and public policies take precedence over religious considerations. In the West, especially in the United States, there is a separation of church and state. Nevertheless, most Indians—including their leaders—have their own self-serving, bizarre definitions. One often cited goes like this: "equal treatment of all the religions by the State." Is that a desirable goal? If it is, then how can any State achieve such a goal?

In the Indian context, I suppose the easiest way for the State to treat all religions "equally" would be to intrude into every religion equally and if need be, somehow proclaim all religions are one and inseparable from Hinduism—thereby making everyone in India a Hindu. This is precisely what is happening in India. Because everyone is a Hindu, the leadership expects a response in kind. It usually shows in an intellectually flawed population which has stamped itself with a bogus notion echoed in the buzzword called "sameness." This is an expression erroneously viewed as synonymous with equality.

Under this framed scenario, the very thought of discrimination or even persecution of one religion by another need not arise since we are all the same—that is, we are all Hindus. Obviously, this kind of an argument carries a heavy price tag. When told that India's sacred Constitution exudes an egalitarian system, years of Hindu conditioning have transfixed the populace to acquiesce to any communiqué coming down from the top. Few will ever fathom that India's egalitarianism is not the same sort we know in a Western sense but is rather of an entirely different substance. It is rooted in the infamous caste system, or in a more precise language, the Hindu apartheid. While the caste system is alive, thriving, and functional, India's Hindu leaders boast of an Indian democracy, ignoring its pervasive underlying segregation and inequality. This sounds magnificently absurd. Many Indian leaders on one hand enjoy the fruits of being born into an elite caste (while most of the population rots at the lowest caste levels), while on the other, they mindlessly sing the gospel of equality.

Because caste is a substructure of Hindu society, talk of "equality," "democracy," and "secularism" reverberates only to mislead the masses. Not surprisingly, this kind of tactical maneuvering to deceive is clear in the Constitution and conspicuous in the State's public policy and internal propaganda.[18] While Sikhs, Jains, and Buddhists have already been "secularized" constitutionally, Christians and Muslims are now also in the process of being "secularized" through state-orchestrated propaganda. Several Indian leaders now call Indian Christians and Muslims as "Christi Hindus" and "Mohammadiya Hindus," respectively. In addition, some provincial State governments inside India have already enacted anti-conversion laws, while others are contemplating ensuring the Hindu population doesn't slide away into something else.

Conclusion

Other amendments of the Bill of Rights in the U.S. Constitution guarantee the American people numerous other fundamental rights. These include right to bear arms (Amendment II); protection against government officials who might invade their homes and seize property without legal permission (Amendment IV); protection against being "a witness against himself" in any criminal case or being "deprived of life, liberty, or property, without due process of law" (Amendment V); the right of a person accused of a crime "to a speedy and public trial by an impartial jury" (Amendment VI); and protection against "cruel and unusual punishments" (Amendment VIII). Can the Constitution of India match the U.S. Bill of Rights word for word? If it cannot, can its intentions at least match those of the U.S. Bill of Rights? If reading articles 19 and 25 has left anyone with a cause for concern, then the remaining portions of Part III of the Indian Constitution should not come as a surprise. After due consideration, it is clear: the Indian Constitution guarantees no fundamental rights—despite the endless rhetoric from India's leaders, its intelligentsia, and its apologists.

Appendix C

Preamble to the Constitution of India

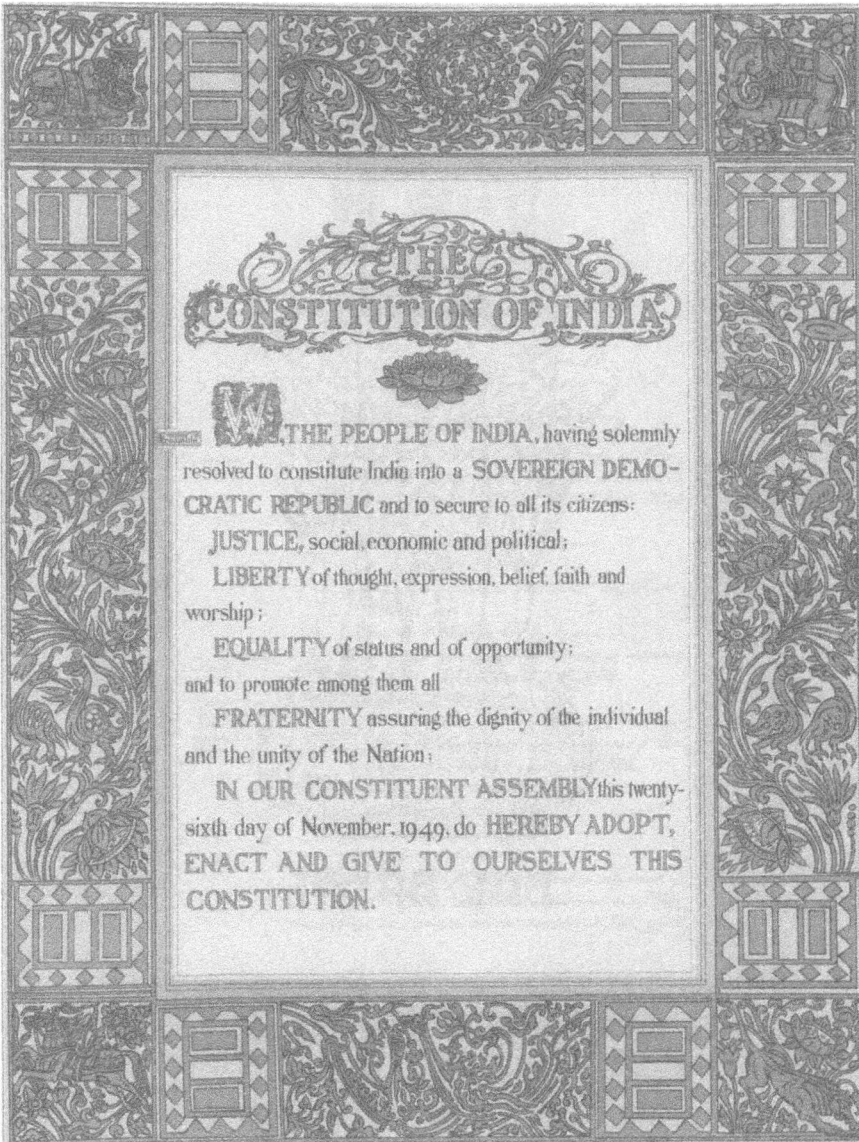

THE

CONSTITUTION OF INDIA

WE, THE PEOPLE OF INDIA, having solemnly resolved to constitute India into a SOVEREIGN DEMO-CRATIC REPUBLIC and to secure to all its citizens:

JUSTICE, social, economic and political;

LIBERTY of thought, expression, belief, faith and worship;

EQUALITY of status and of opportunity; and to promote among them all

FRATERNITY assuring the dignity of the individual and the unity of the Nation;

IN OUR CONSTITUENT ASSEMBLY this twenty-sixth day of November, 1949, do HEREBY ADOPT, ENACT AND GIVE TO OURSELVES THIS CONSTITUTION.

Figure B: Preamble to the Constitution of India

Appendix D

List of Illustrations in the Constitution of India

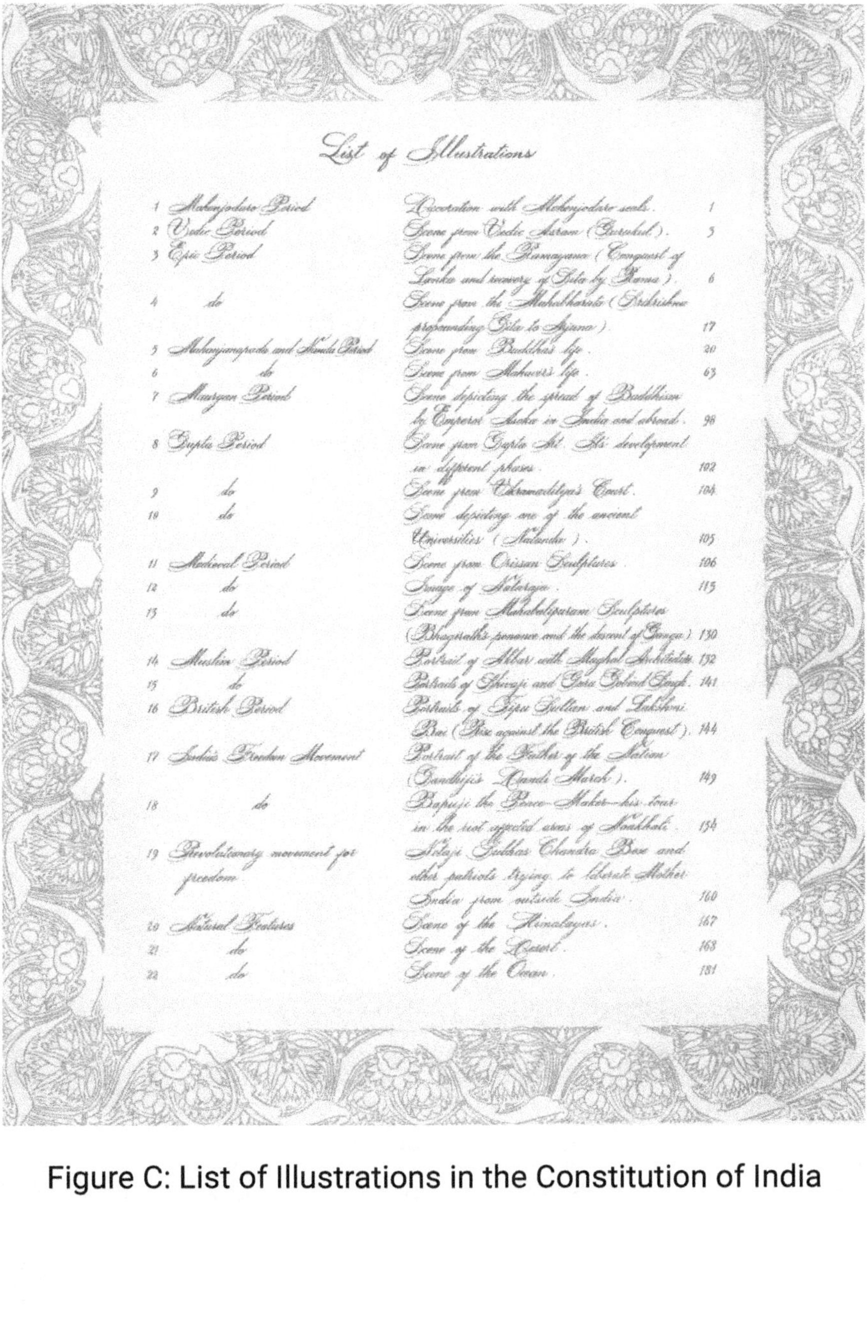

List of Illustrations

Figure C: List of Illustrations in the Constitution of India

Table of Illustrations

		Preamble
Part I	Mohenjodaro Period	Decoration with Mohenjodaro Seals
Part II	Vedic Period	Scene from Vedic Asram (Gurukul)
Part III	Epic Period	Scene from the Ramayana (Conquest of Lanka and recovery of Sita by Rama)
Part IV	Do	Scene from the Mahabharata (Srikrishna propounding Gita to Arjuna)
Part V	Mahanjanapada and Nanda Period	Scene from Buddha's life
Part VI	Do	Scene from Mahavir's life
Part VII	Mauryan Period	Scene depicting the spread of Buddhism by Emperor Asoka in India and abroad
Part VIII	Gupta Period	Scene from Gupta Art. Its development in different phases
Part IX	Do	Scene from Vikramaditya's Court
Part X	Do	Scene depicting one of the ancient Universities (Nalanda)
Part XI	Medieval Period	Scene from Orissan Sculptures
Part XII	Do	Image of Nataraja
Part XIII	Do	Scene from Mahabalipuram Sculptures
Part XIV	Muslim Period	Portrait of Akbar and Mughal Architecture

Part XV	Do	Portraits of Shivaji and Guru Gobind Singh
Part XVI	British Period	Portraits of Tipu Sultan and Lakshmi Bai (Rise against the British Conquest)
Part XVII	India's Freedom Movement	Portrait of the Father of the Nation (Gandhi's Dandi March)
Part XVIII	Do	Bapuji the Peace-Maker – his tour in the riot affected areas of Noakhali
Part XIX	Revolutionary movement for freedom	Netaji Subhash Chandra Bose and other patriots trying to liberate Mother India from outside India
Part XX	Natural Features	Scene of the Himalayas
Part XXI	Do	Scene of the Desert
Part XXII	Do	Scene of the Ocean

Appendix E

Illustrations in the Constitution of India

This Appendix has twenty-two illustrations.   Each illustration marks the first page of a Part of the Constitution.   For example, Figure 1 represents the front page of Part I. Part VII represented here by Figure 7 was repealed in its entirety by the Seventh Amendment Act in 1956.

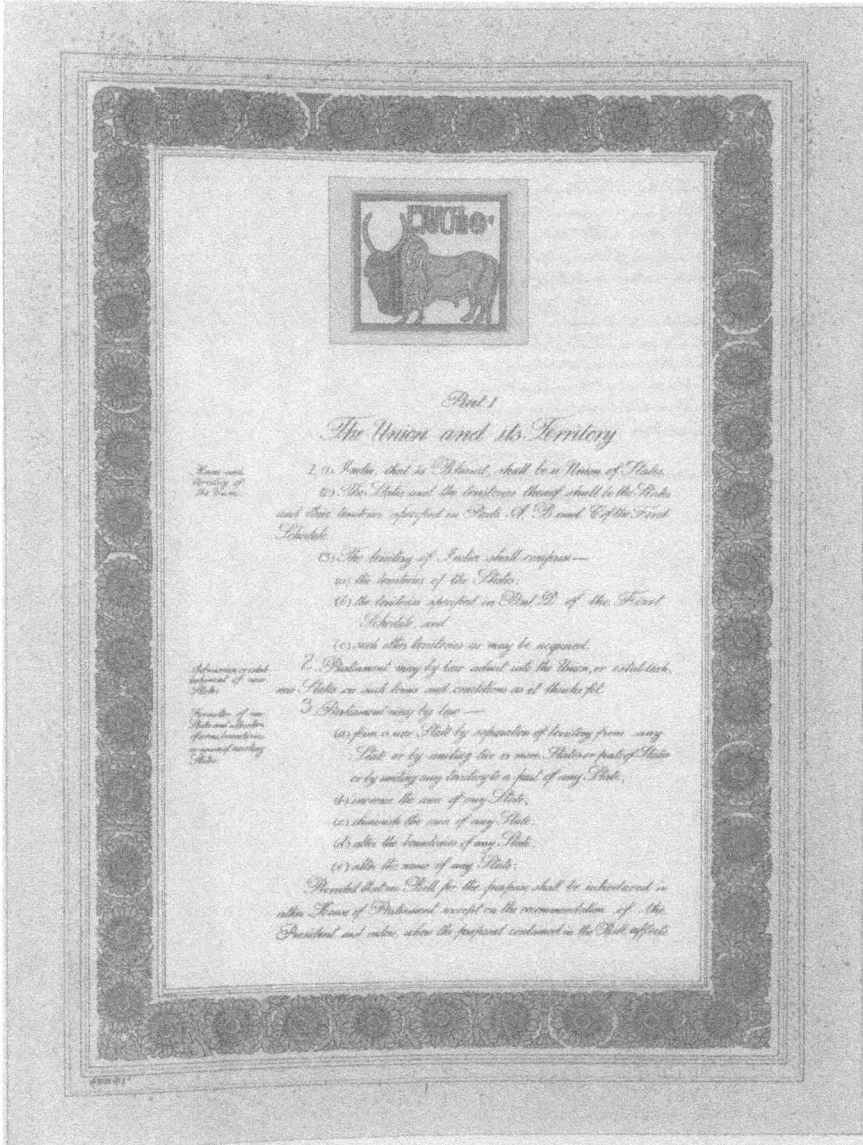

Figure 1: Decoration with Mohenjodaro Seals

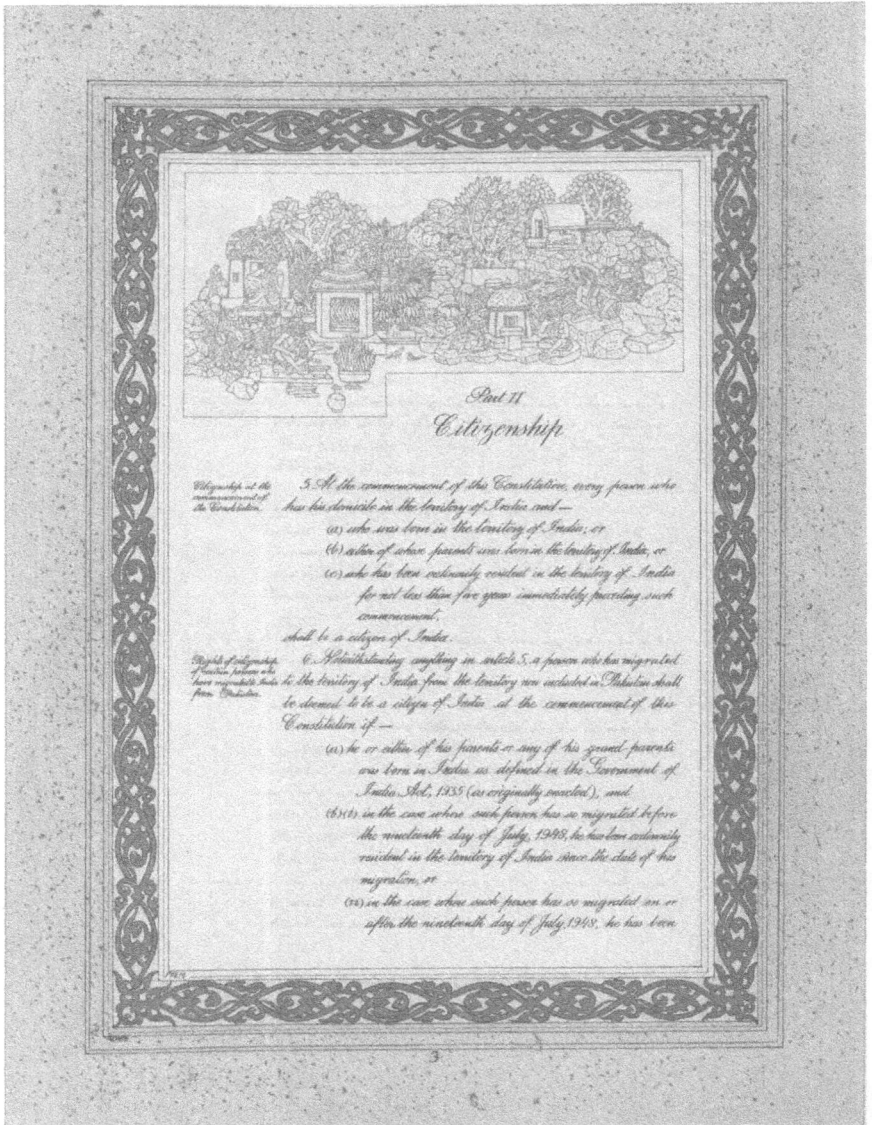

Figure 2: Scene from Vedic Asram (Gurukul)

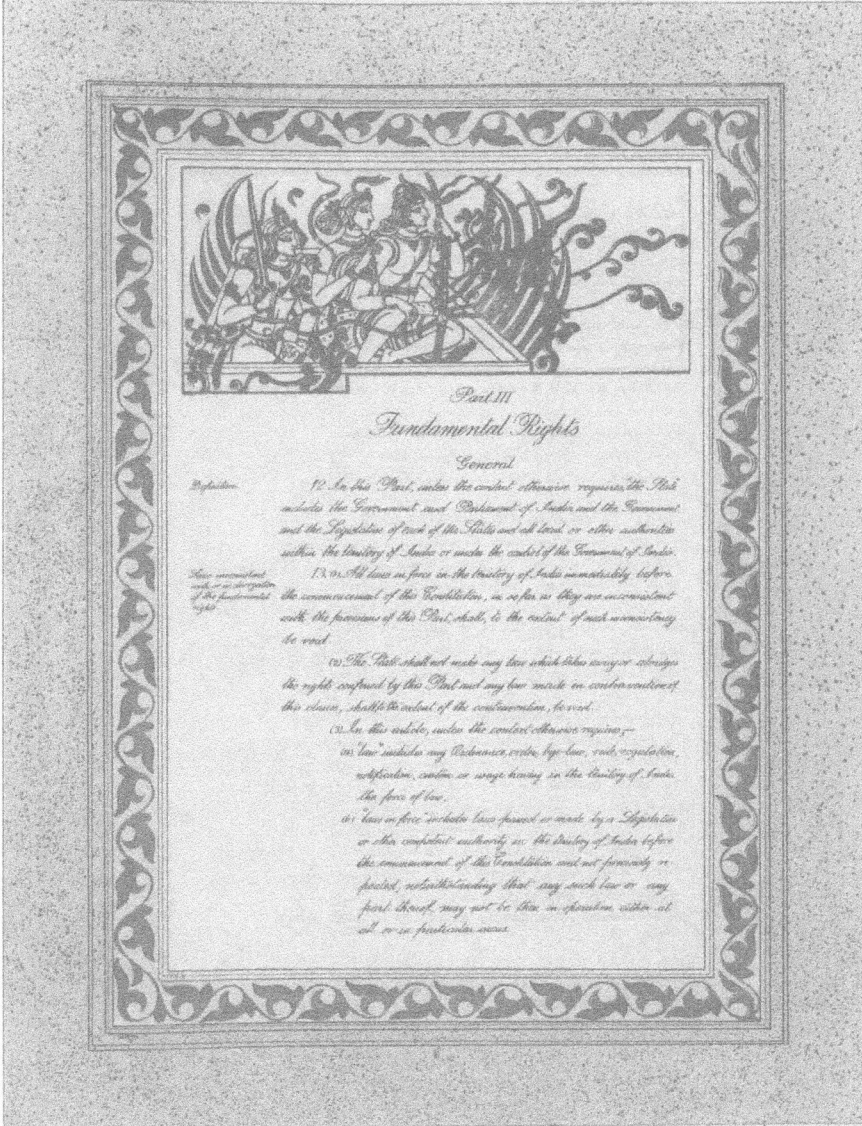

Figure 3: Scene from the Ramayana (Conquest of Lanka and recovery of Sita by Rama)

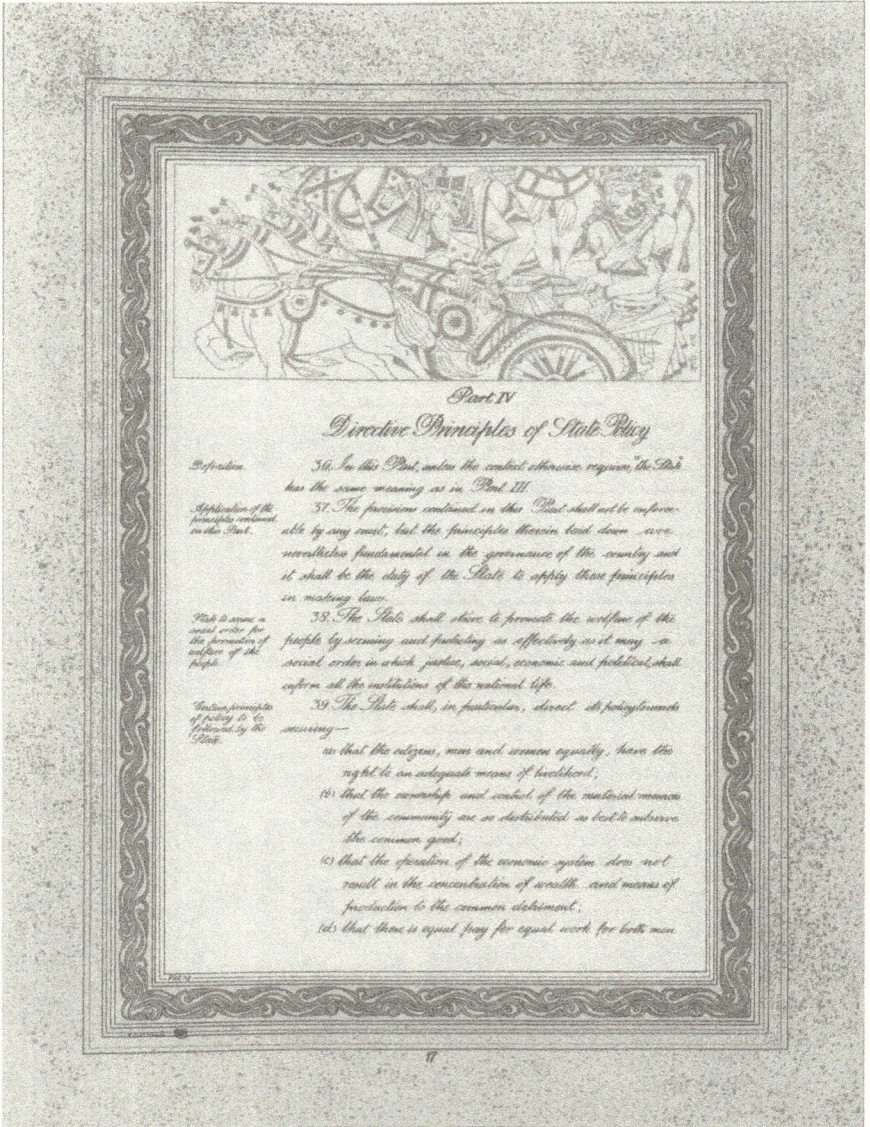

Figure 4: Scene from the Mahabharata (Srikrishna propounding Gita to Arjuna)

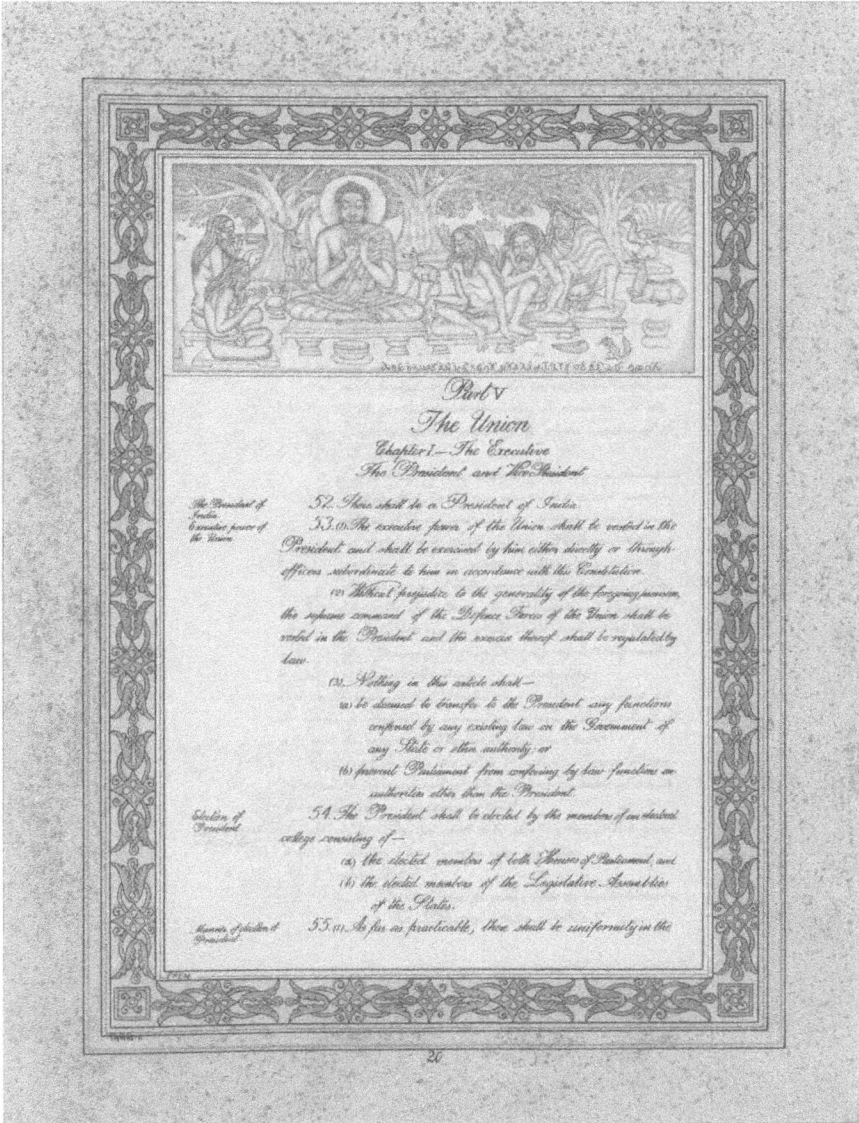

Figure 5: Scene from Buddha's life

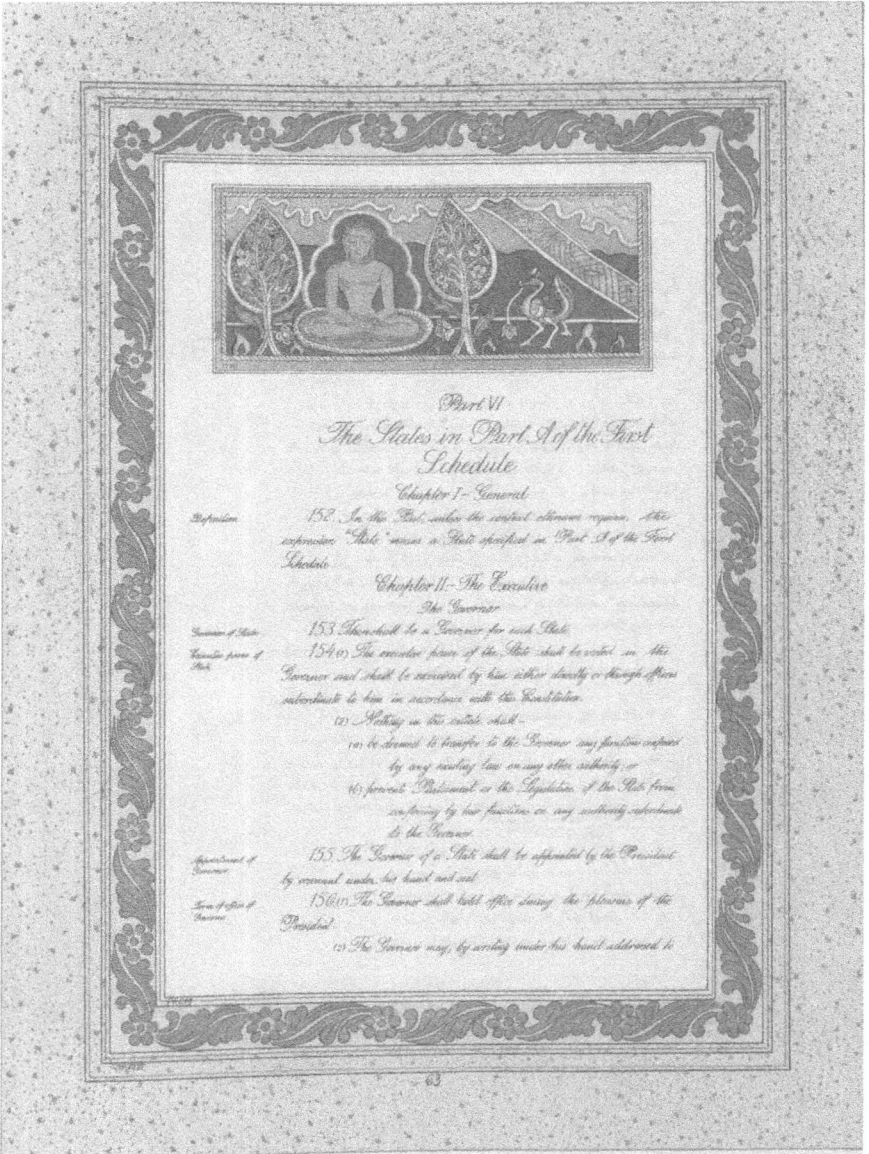

Figure 6: Scene from Mahavir's life

Figure 7: Scene depicting the spread of Buddhism by Emperor Asoka in India and abroad

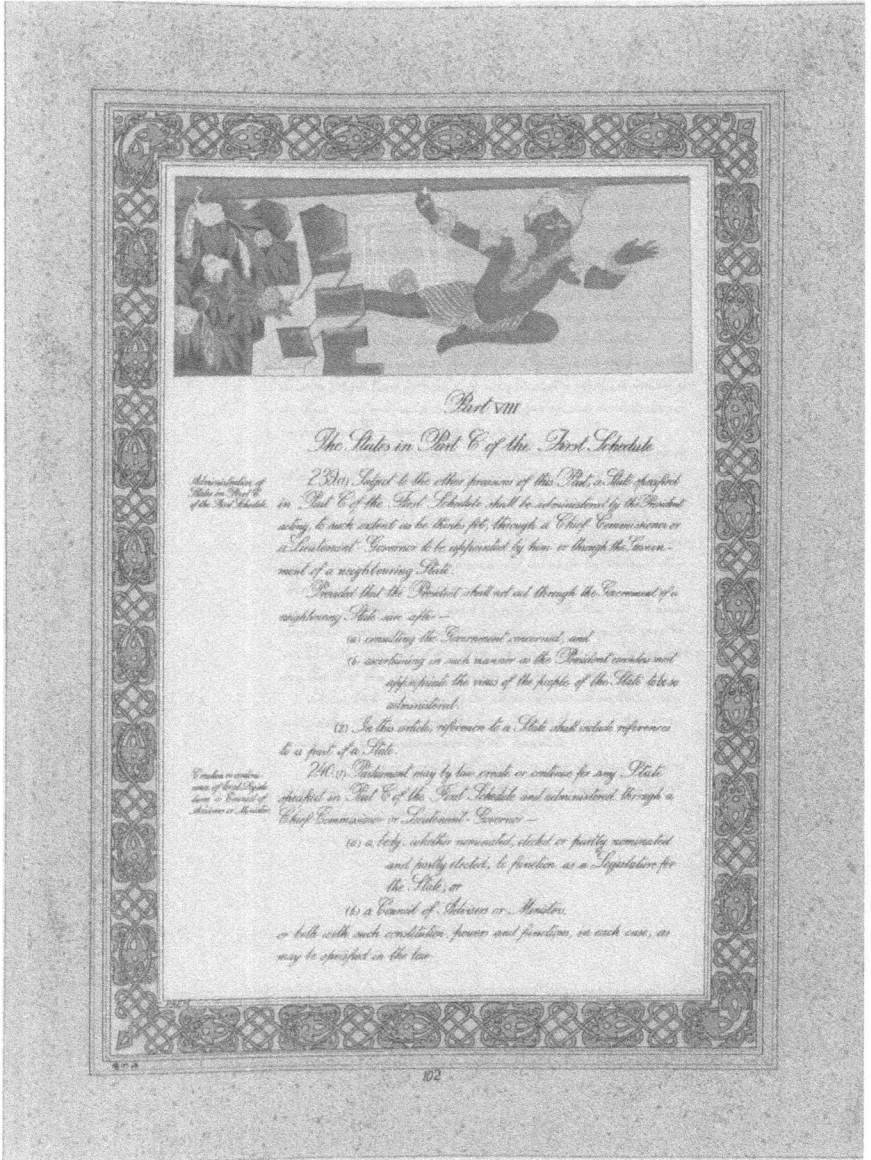

Figure 8: Scene from Gupta Art. Its development in different phases

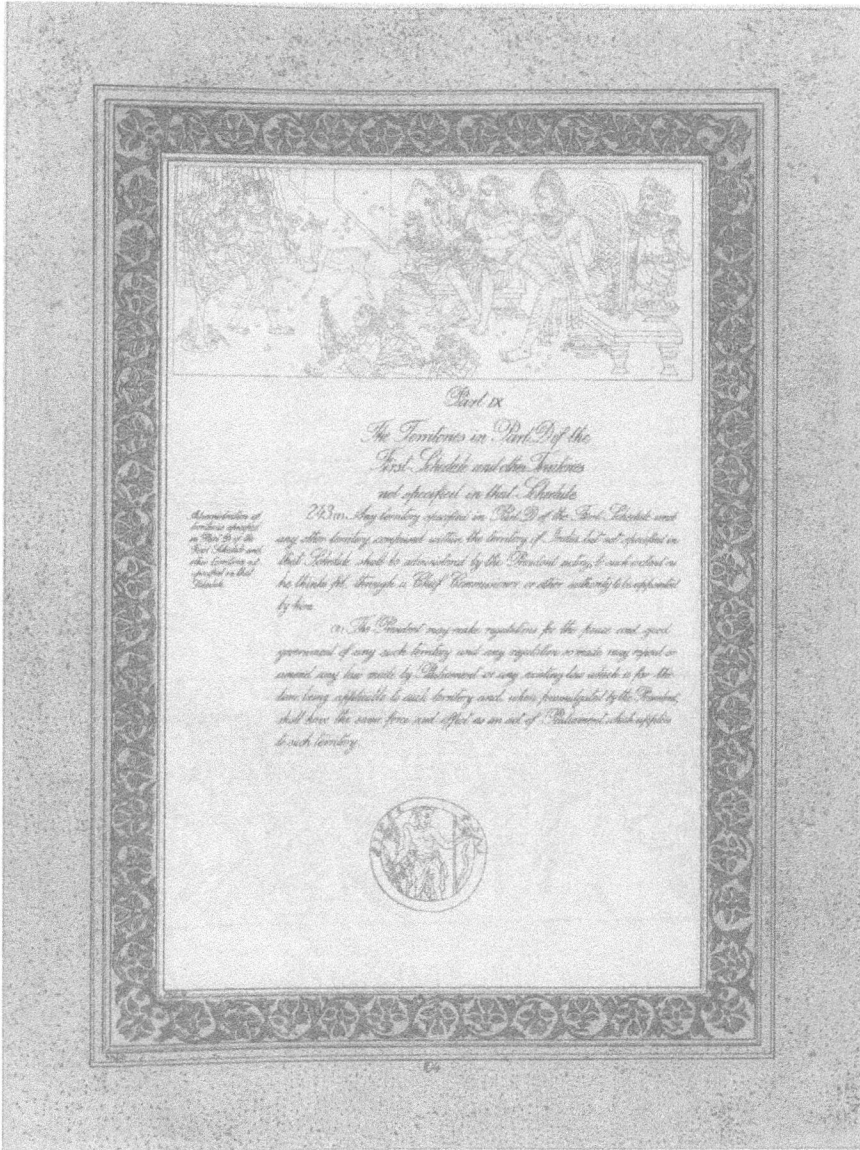

Figure 9: Scene from Vikramaditya's Court

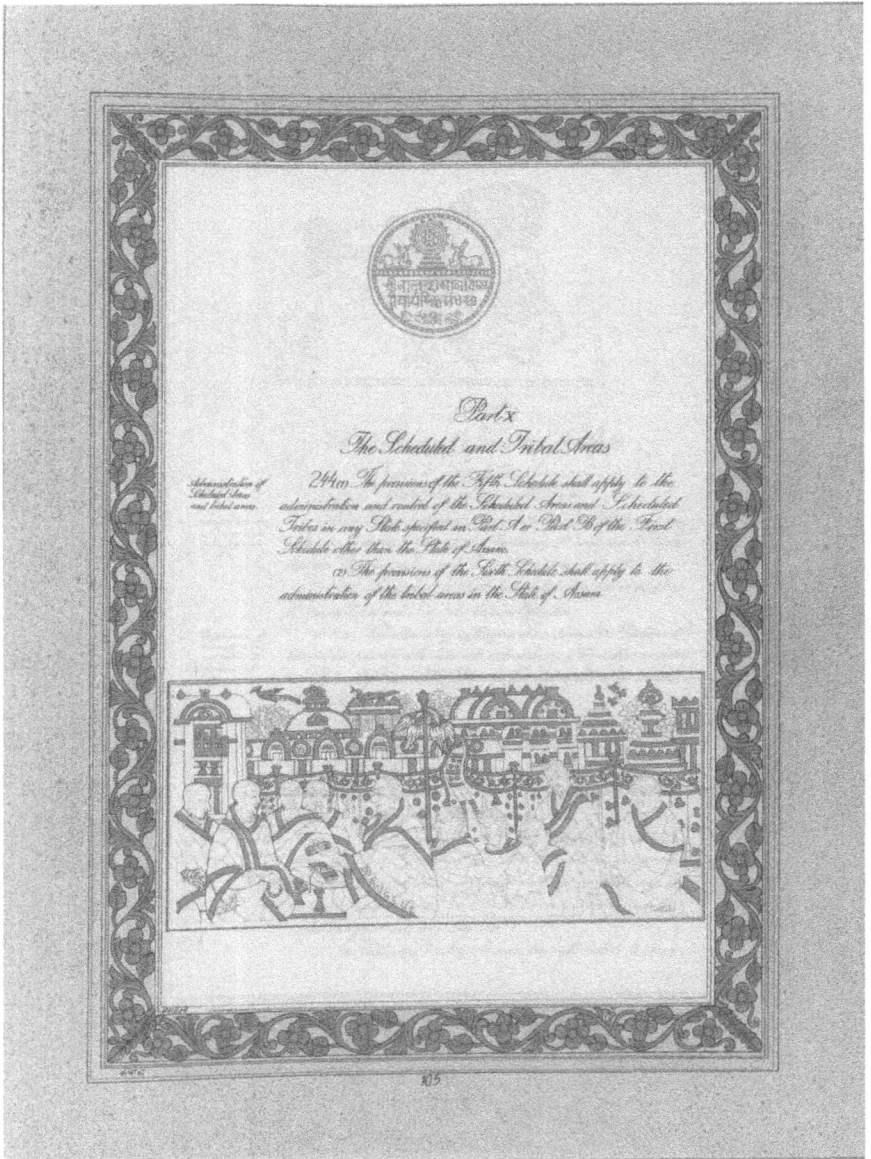

Figure 10: Scene depicting one of the ancient Universities (Nalanda)

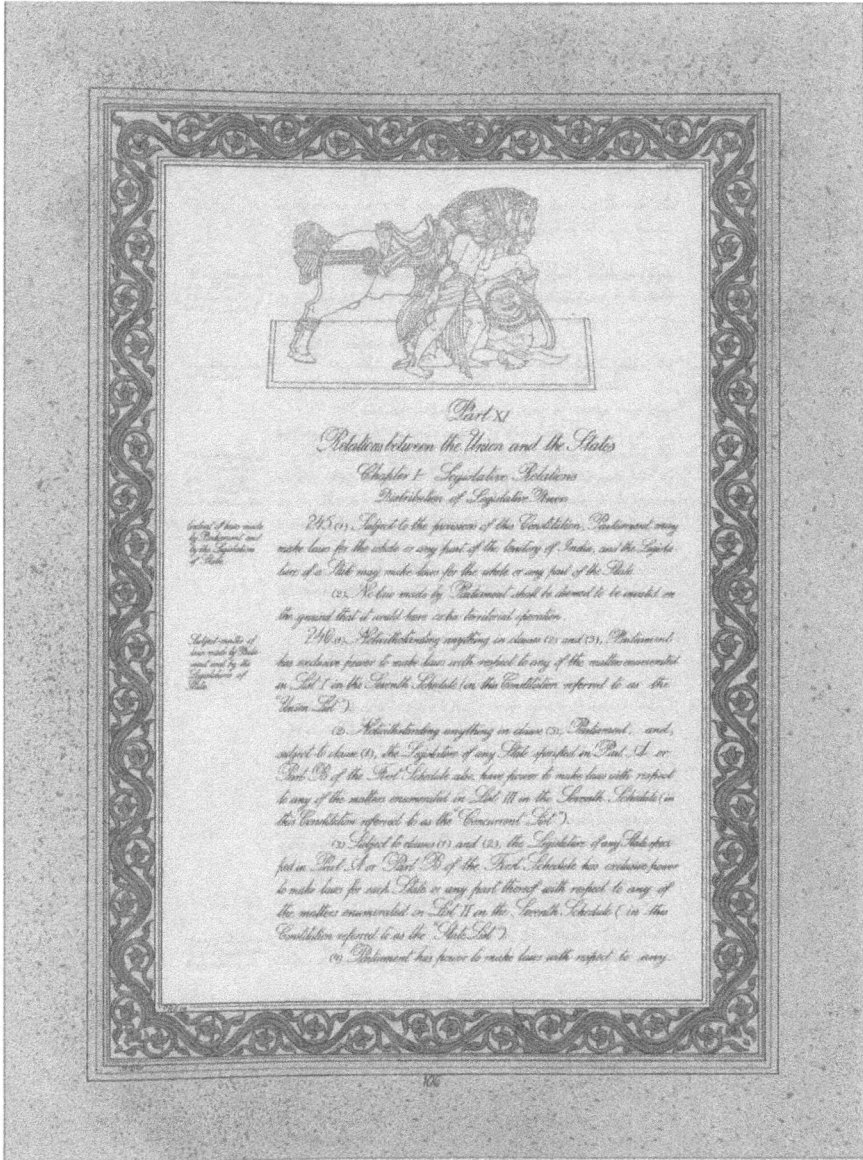

Figure 11: Scene from Orissan Sculptures

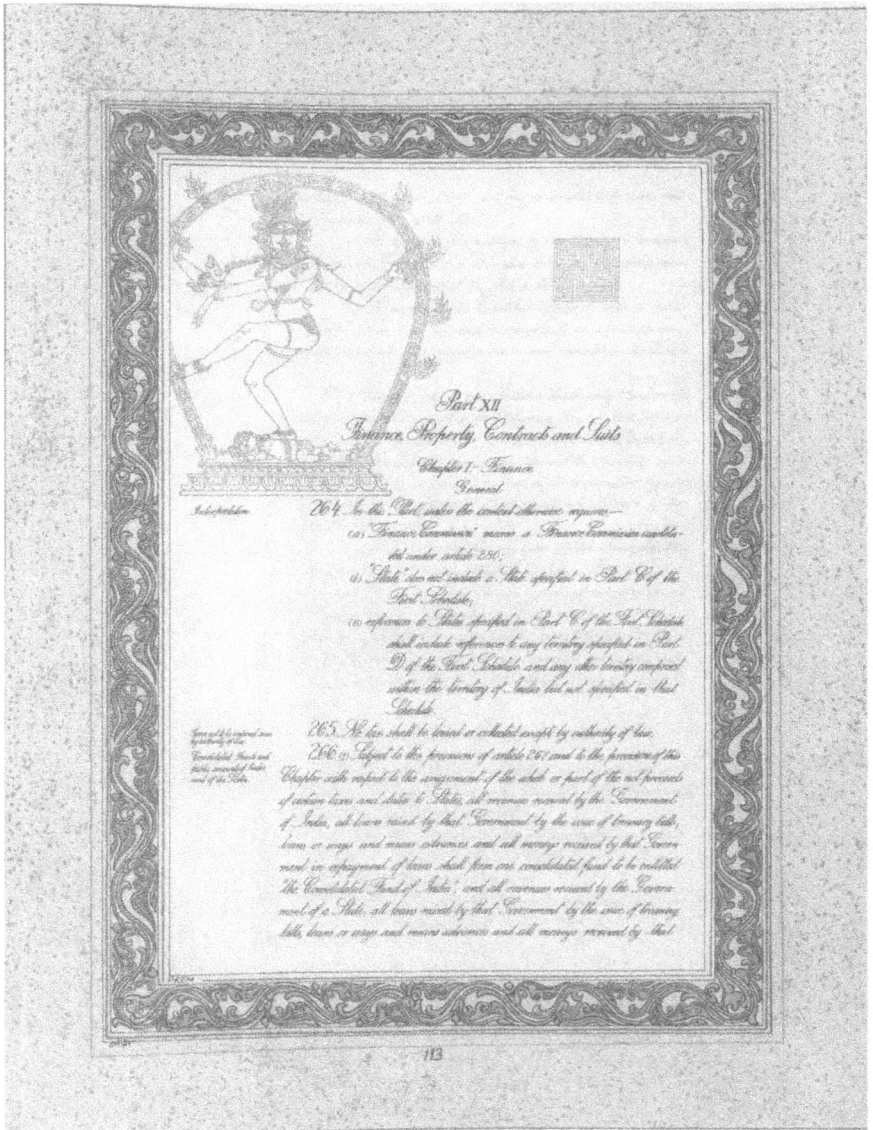

Figure 12: Image of Nataraja

Figure 13: Scene from Mahabalipuram Sculptures

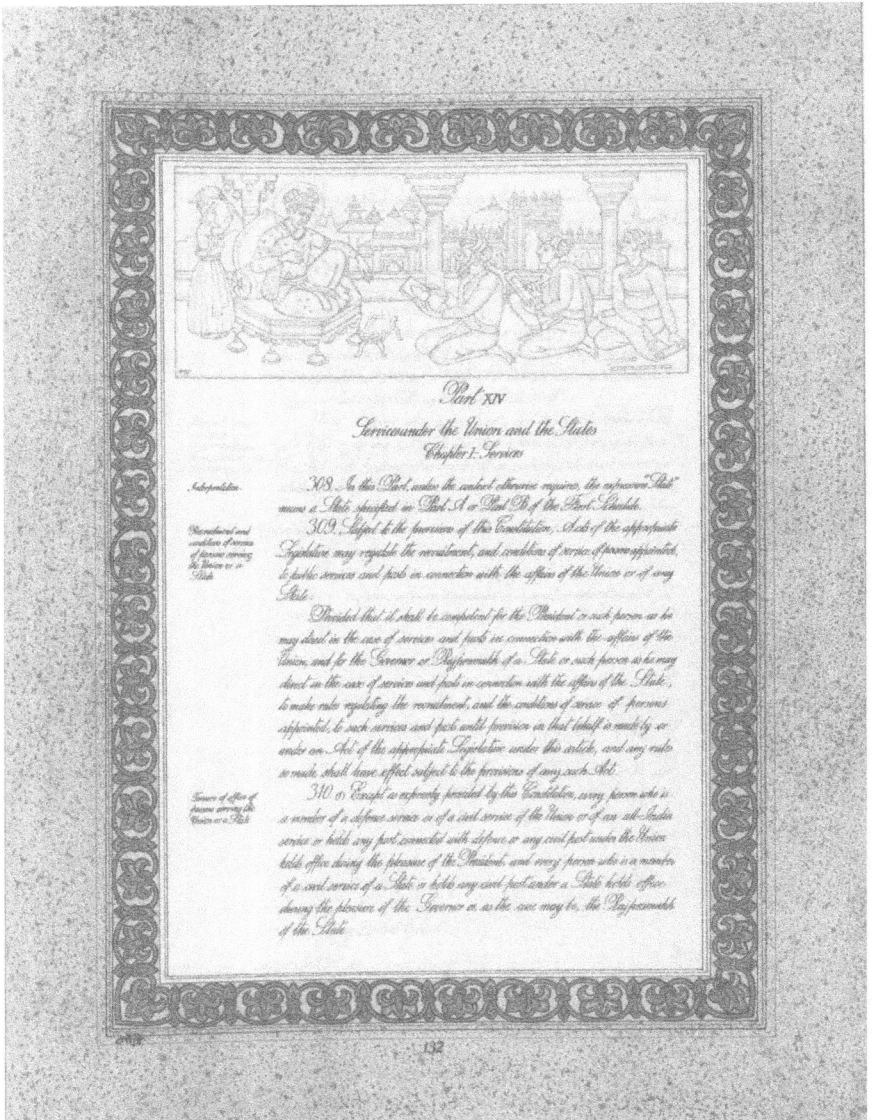

Figure 14: Portrait of Akbar and Mughal Architecture

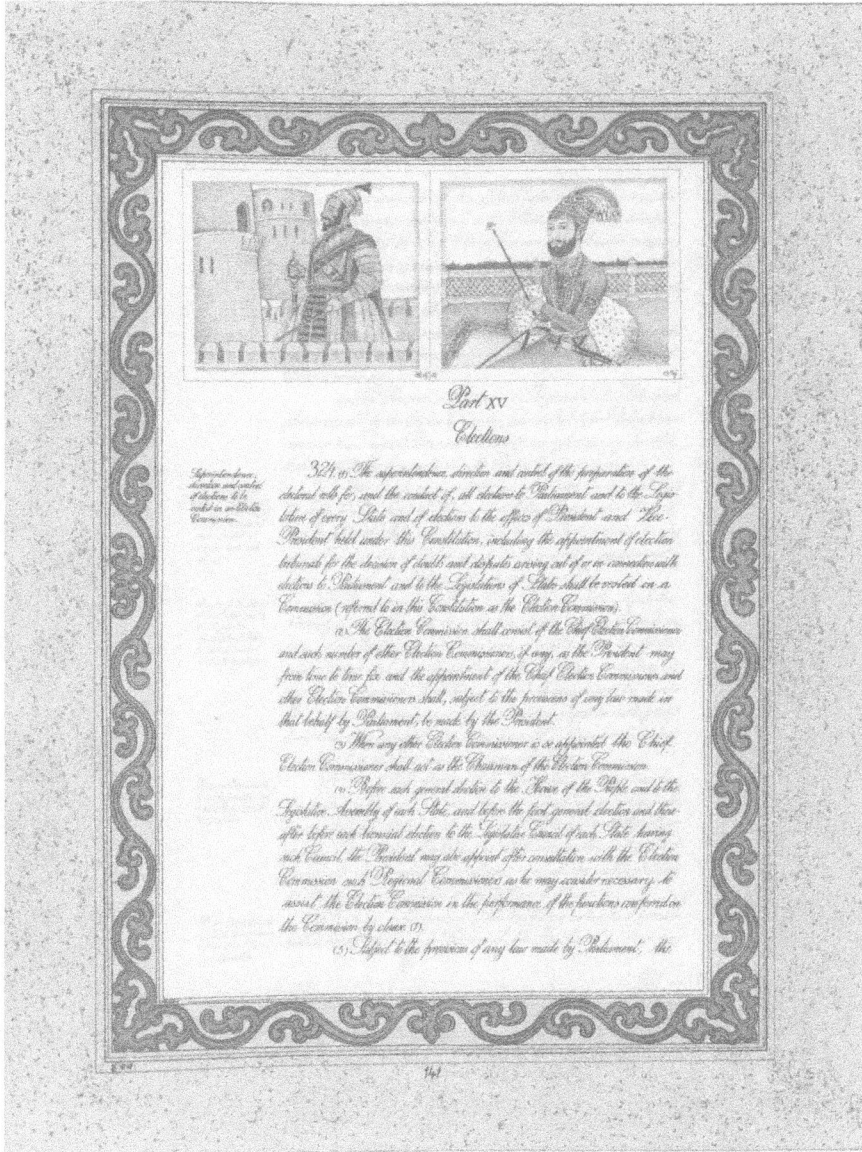

Figure 15: Portraits of Shivaji and Guru Gobind Singh

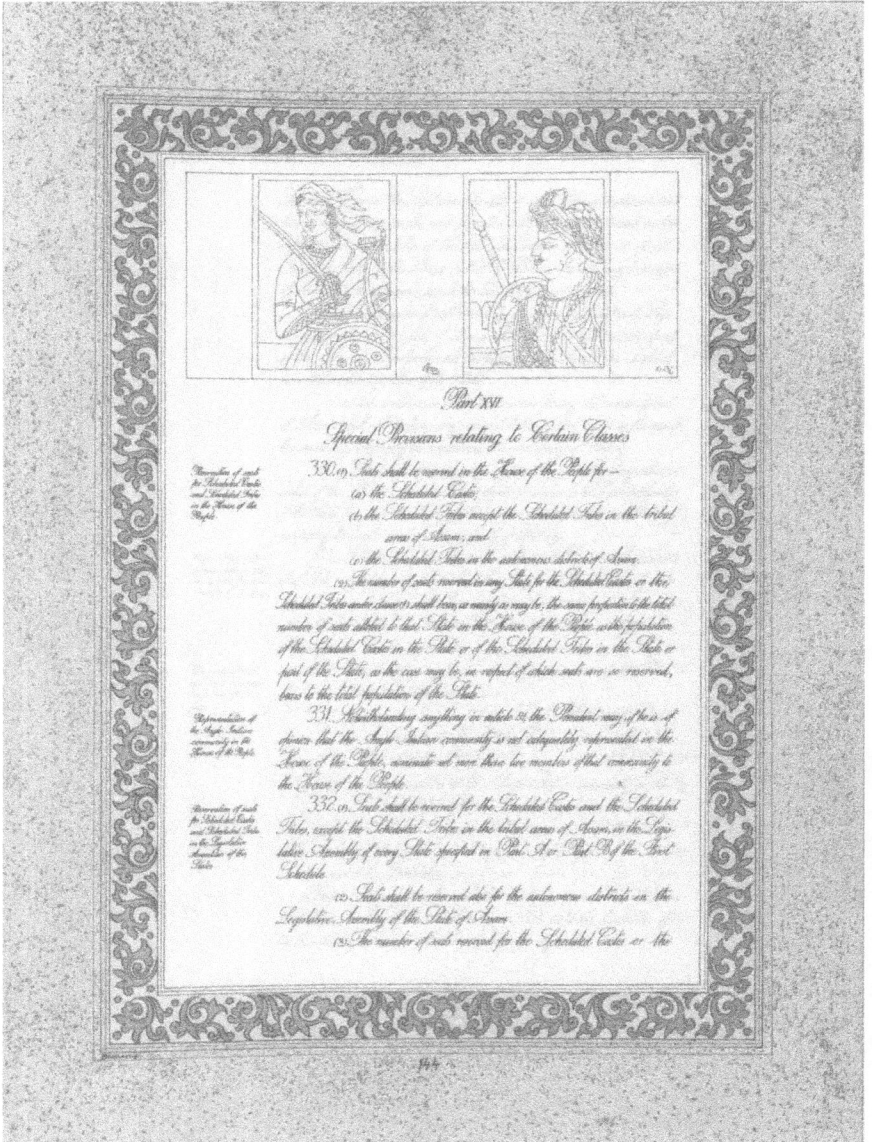

Figure 16: Portraits of Tipu Sultan and Lakshmi Bai (Rise against the British Conquest)

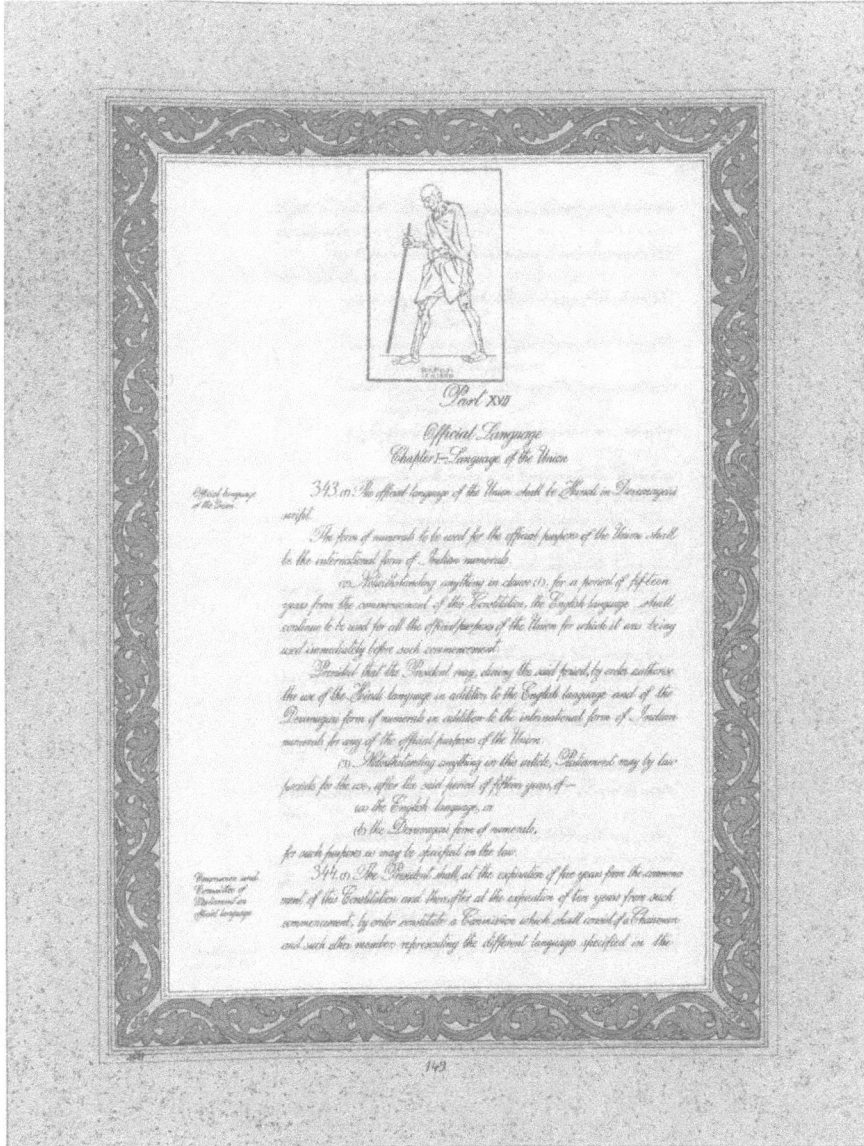

Figure 17: Portrait of the Father of the Nation (Gandhi's Dandi March)

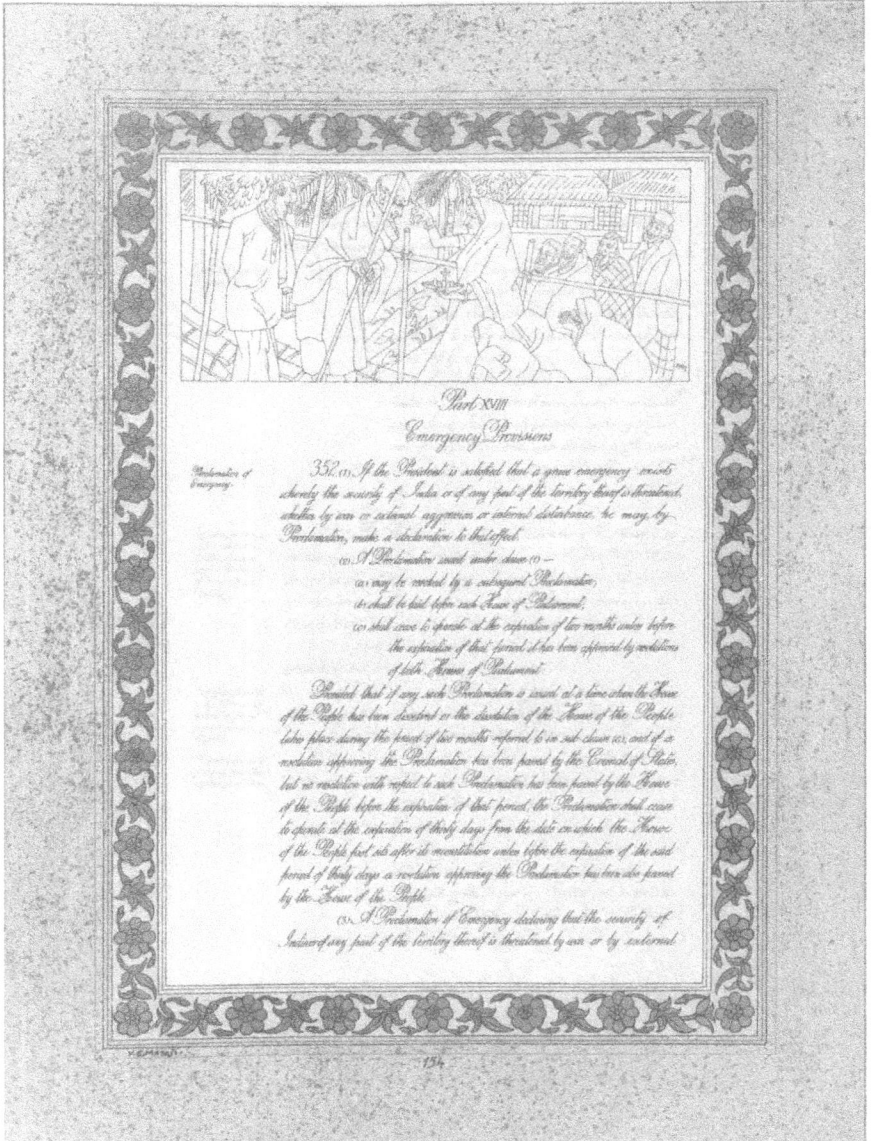

Figure 18: Bapuji the Peace-Maker — his tour in the riot affected areas of Noakhali

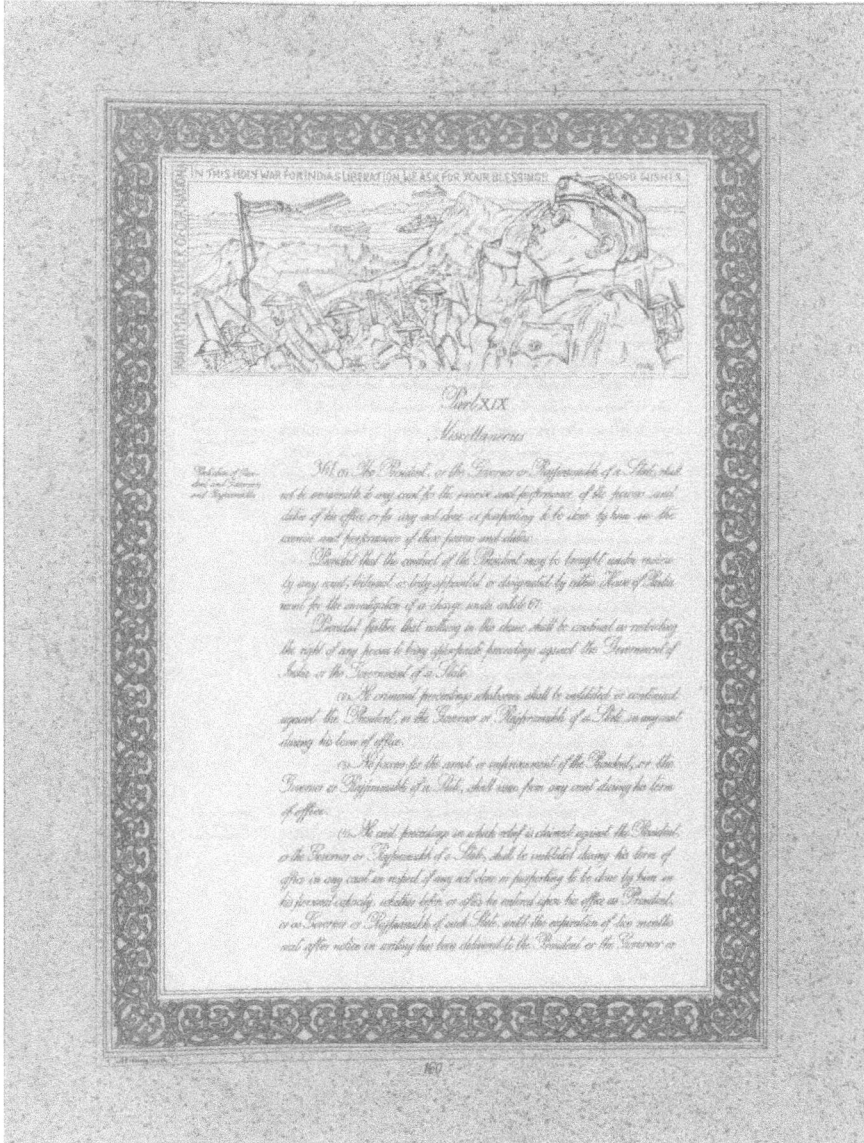

Figure 19: Netaji Subhash Chandra Bose and other patriots trying to liberate Mother India from outside India

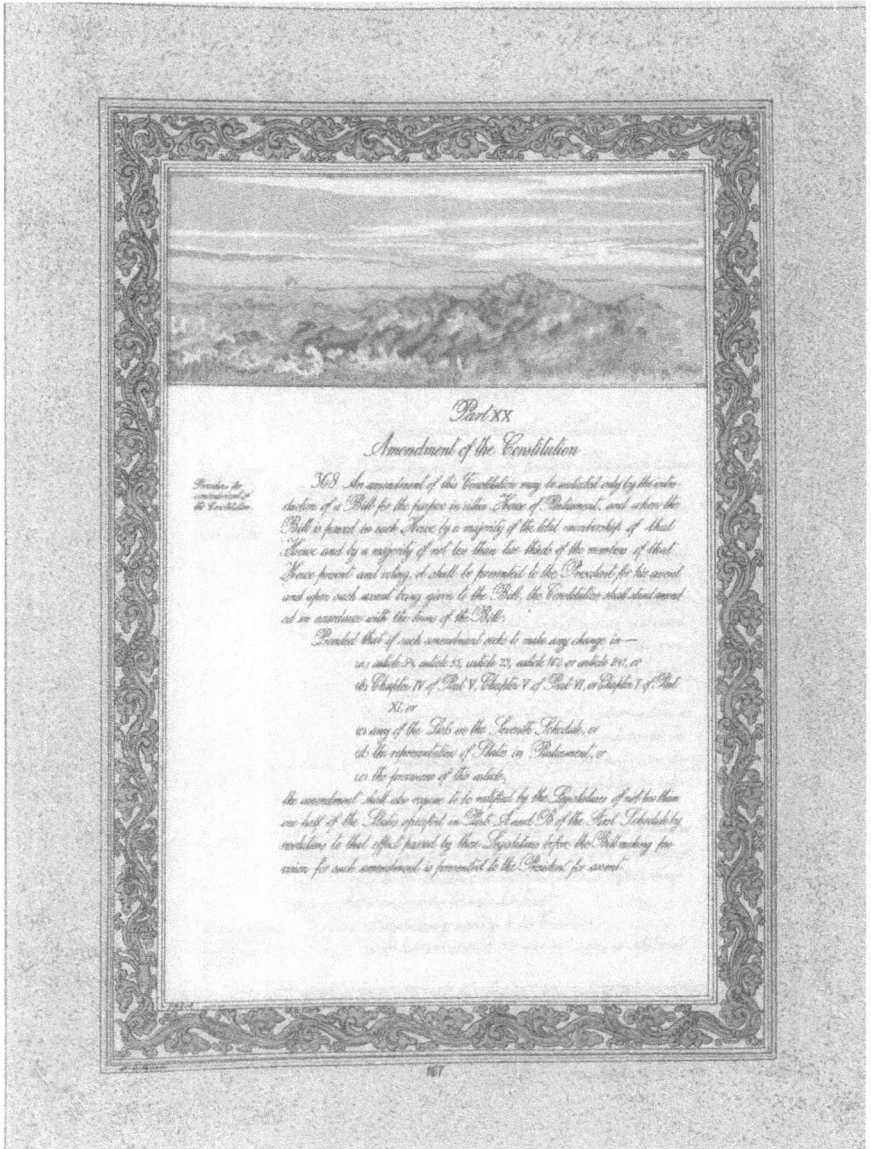

Figure 20: Scene of the Himalayas

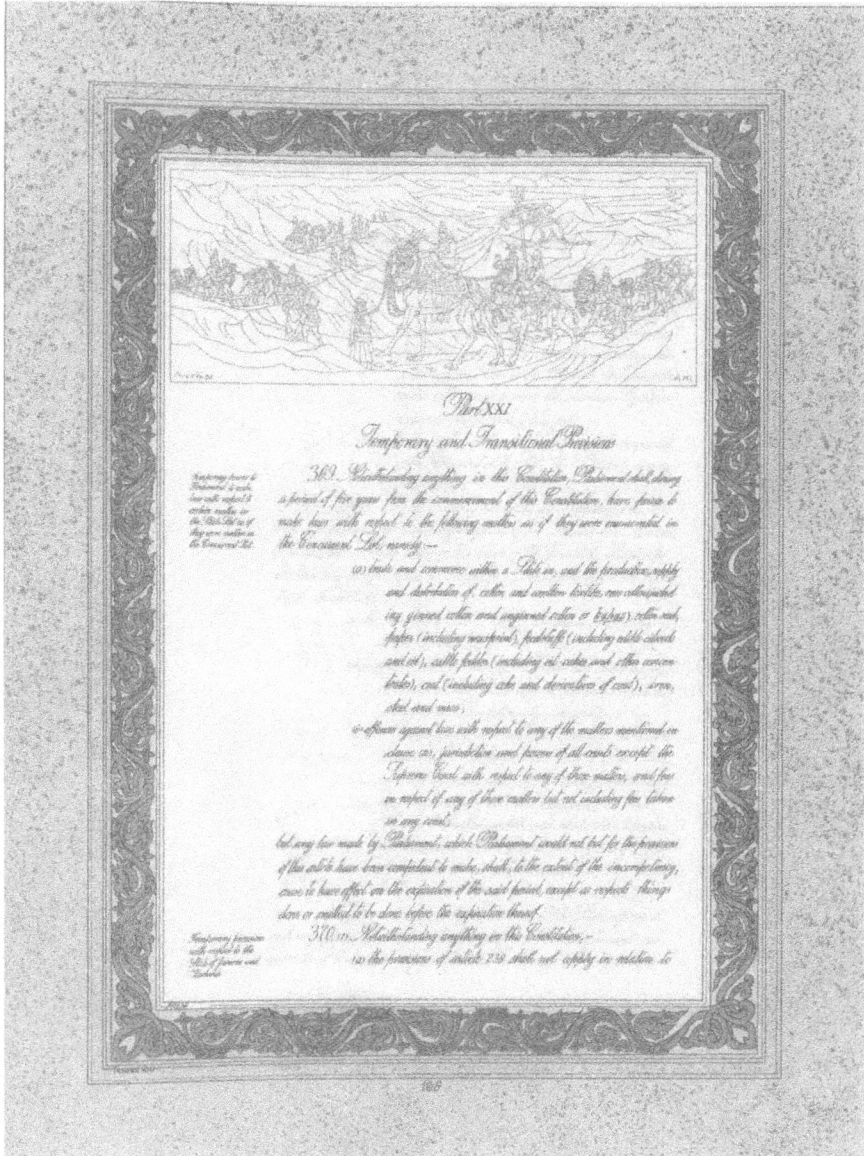

Figure 21: Scene of the Desert

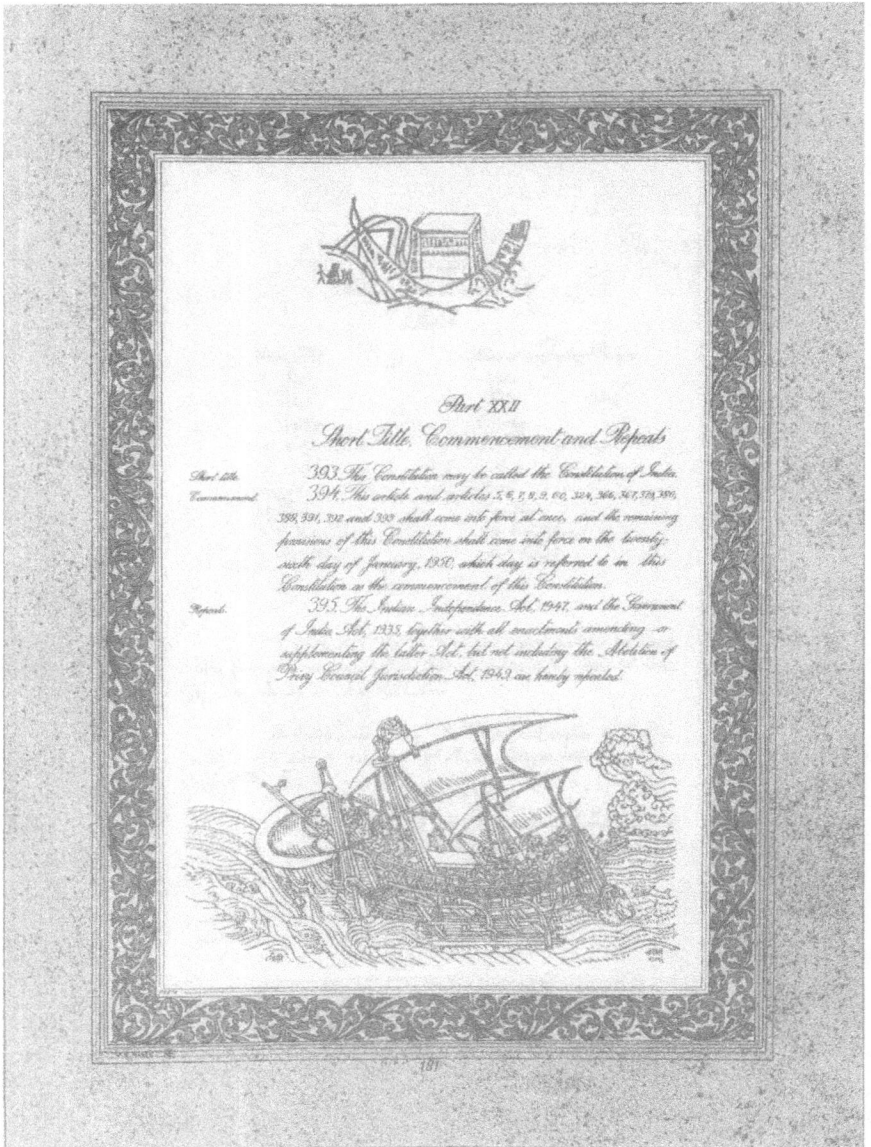

Figure 22: Scene of the Ocean

Notes

[1] In the Hindu caste-system, the Untouchables are a group of people who are placed at the very bottom of the hierarchy. They are often referred to as the black people of India.

[2] The words of Dr. Ambedkar as well as the Constitution of India are spelled in British English in the originals. Such words are reproduced here without change.

[3] The question of how these rights are interpreted by the Supreme Court of India is outside the scope of this book.

[4] For an extended discussion on the caste system, refer to Appendix B.

[5] Article 75(3) states: "The Council of Ministers shall be collectively responsible to the House of the People." Strange use of words, isn't it? In light of the fact that members of Lok Sabha are under control, what does "collectively responsible" really mean?

[6] State Assembly, State Legislature, and Legislature of the State are essentially the same entity.

[7] Kumar, Mukesh. (2010). "Discretionary Powers of the Governor under the Constitution of India" (Doctoral Dissertation Presented to the Faculty of Law of the Punjabi University). Retrieved from http://shodhganga.inflibnet.ac.in/handle/10603/3695.

[8] In a 1953 interview with British Broadcasting Corporation, Dr. Ambedkar responded to a question concerning the sham election system:

> BBC: But elections are important because they give chance to change the government.
>
> Dr. Ambedkar: Yes, but who has an idea that voting means the change of the government? Nobody has. People have no consciousness and our electoral system never allows [us] to choose the candidate ...

Retrieved from: velivada.com on December 27, 2017.

[9] Article 356 allows the President to assume the functions of the government of a State if he/she "is satisfied that a situation has arisen in which the Government of the State cannot be carried on in accordance with the provisions of this Constitution."

[10] Reading the pages of the Constituent Assembly Debates in Vol. XI, we learn that both the Socialist Party of India (Drafting Constitution of Indian Republic) and the Hindu Mahasabha (Constitution of the Hindustan Free

State) pitched in by writing their respective books (in red by the Socialists) to influence the Constituent Assembly.

[11] For an extended discussion of Gandhism, we recommend the following two books: *Gandhi: Behind the Mask of Divinity*. Amherst, NY: Prometheus Books, 2004, and *Gandhi Under Cross-Examination*. Lathrop, CA: Sovereign Star Publishing, 2009.

[12] *Sathapatha Brahmana* is a Hindu sacred text (one among many) which describes details of Vedic rituals, including the fascinating background of mythological narratives.

[13] In support of his anti-constitution views, Dr. Ambedkar in an interview held in May 1956 with Michael Brecher made it quite clear that it was the stalwarts [Congress Party 's Caucus] of the Indian National Congress who were the actual decision makers regarding what entered the copy of the draft constitution. Their instructions were translated into the constitutional language and then incorporated into the draft copy of the constitution by the drafting committee. This interview makes it crystal clear that Dr. Ambedkar was not the author of India's Constitution. (See – *Nehru: A Political Biography*; London: Oxford University Press, 1959. Page 423)

[14] This is an adaptation and somewhat edited form of an earlier article published in the August 2009 issue New English Review, an online magazine. This article in its earliest version was published in Sikhspectrum.com during 2003-2004.

[15] I am indebted to Professor Marc Galanter who has written the chapter titled: "Hinduism, Secularism and the Indian Judiciary" in the book *Secularism and its Critics* edited by Rajiv Bhargava.

[16] This analysis is distilled from India's Supreme Court case: *Shastri Yagnapurushdasji v. Muldas Bhandardas Vaishya*, AIR 1966 SC 1119; [1966] 3 SCR 242 [5 Judge Bench] [P.B. Gajendragadkar, Chief Justice]

[17] Samaraditya Pal. *India's Constitution: Origin and Evolution*, Volume 2, LexisNexis; Gurgaon, Haryana, 2015, pages 959-960.

[18] For further study we recommend two books: M.P. Raju. *India's Constitution: Roots, Values & Wrongs*. Delhi: Media House, 2017, and S.P. Singh Chauhan. *Sources and Framing of The Constitution of India with Special Reference to Vedic Governance*. New Delhi, India: Universal Law Publishing Co. Pvt. Ltd., 2015.

Authors

ANMOL SINGH is a Software Engineer working in California. In addition, he is a student of Indian politics and religion.

G.B. SINGH is a retired U.S. Army officer. He is the author of the books: *Gandhi: Behind the Mask of Divinity*. Amherst, NY: Prometheus Books, 2004, and *Gandhi Under Cross-Examination*. Lathrop, CA: Sovereign Star Publishing, 2009.

www.ingramcontent.com/pod-product-compliance
Lightning Source LLC
Chambersburg PA
CBHW022112280326
41933CB00007B/347